CRITICAL PERSPECTIVES ON

GENDER IDENTITY

ANALYZING THE ISSUES

CRITICAL PERSPECTIVES ON
GENDER IDENTITY

Edited by Nicki Peter Petrikowski

Enslow Publishing

101 W. 23rd Street
Suite 240
New York, NY 10011
USA

enslow.com

Published in 2017 by Enslow Publishing, LLC
101 W. 23rd Street, Suite 240, New York, NY 10011

Library of Congress Cataloging-in-Publication Data

Names: Petrikowski, Nicki Peter, editor.
Title: Critical perspectives on gender identity / edited by Nicki Peter
  Petrikowski.
Description: New York, NY : Enslow Publishing, 2017. | Series: Analyzing
the issues | Includes bibliographical references and index.
Identifiers: LCCN 2015050628 | ISBN 9780766076723 (library bound)
Subjects: LCSH: Transgender people—Juvenile literature. | Transgender
  people—Identity—Juvenile literature. | Transgender people—Legal status,
  laws, etc.—Juvenile literature. | Gender identity—Juvenile literature.
Classification: LCC HQ77.9 .C75 2017 | DDC 306.76/8—dc23
LC record available at http://lccn.loc.gov/2015050628

Printed in the United States of America

To Our Readers: We have done our best to make sure all website addresses in this book were active and appropriate when we went to press. However, the author and the publisher have no control over and assume no liability for the material available on those websites or on any websites they may link to. Any comments or suggestions can be sent by e-mail to customerservice@enslow.com.

Excerpts and articles have been reproduced with the permission of the copyright holders.

Photo Credits: Cover, Alex Wong/Getty Images News/Getty Images ("pass ENDA" demonstration), Thaiview/Shutterstock.com (background, pp. 6–7 background), gbreezy/Shutterstock.com (magnifying glass on spine); p. 6 Ghornstern/Shutterstock.com (header design element, chapter start background throughout book.

CONTENTS

INTRODUCTION 6

CHAPTER 1
WHAT THE EXPERTS SAY 8

CHAPTER 2
WHAT THE GOVERNMENT AND CHURCH
LEADERS SAY... 39

CHAPTER 3
WHAT THE COURTS SAY 79

CHAPTER 4
WHAT ADVOCACY GROUPS SAY 109

CHAPTER 5
WHAT THE MEDIA SAY 134

CHAPTER 6
WHAT ORDINARY PEOPLE SAY.............. 159

CONCLUSION 189
BIBLIOGRAPHY..................................... 190
CHAPTER NOTES................................... 193
GLOSSARY 197
FOR MORE INFORMATION.................... 199
INDEX 201
ABOUT THE EDITOR............................. 207

INTRODUCTION

Most cisgender people—those whose gender agrees with the sex they were assigned at birth—probably don't think much about their own gender identity. Why should they spare a thought about something that they take entirely for granted? The way they feel inside about their gender aligns with the gender they were assigned at birth, which they accept as a matter of course. Society reinforces the norm that a person is either male or female, corresponding to specific physical traits, and there are expectations in regard to a person's behavior and expression depending on their gender. These expectations loom large from the day we are born, and most people think nothing of it that boys are supposed to wear blue and play with cars while girls are supposed to wear pink and play with dolls. In the minds of many people, this is the way it has always been and the way it should be, although there is no obvious reason for it. And challenging this widely accepted order of things can be difficult.

For some people, the question of gender identity plays a far greater role because they do not fit into the narrowly defined categories many accept as the norm. They do not identify as the gender they were assigned at birth. Some people may identify as male although they were born with female reproductive organs, and some may identify as female although they were born with male physical traits.

We call people whose gender identity goes beyond our binary categories of male or female "transgender." Transgender people can also self-identify as something in-between—or something entirely different from the cultural norms of male and female. To these individuals, it is clear that the gender binary society has created does not properly reflect their realities. In many situations, from something simple like the use of public restrooms to more complicated matters like employment and health insurance, there is no room for transgender people who do not fit the cultural norms of male or female gender. Not fitting into one of these two categories can cause anxiety and depression, and lead to an overwhelming sense of isolation. It is very hard to be different from what society expects one to be. Since humans generally fear what they do not understand, this frequently leads to discrimination and even violence.

Gender nonconforming individuals have existed throughout all of human history. In some societies they were accepted, while in Western culture they have generally been ostracized. Only in recent years has the question of gender identity gained more visibility. Transgender characters in popular TV shows have brought the topic to the attention of a wider audience, and many follow the stories of celebrities coming out as transgender with interest. Unfortunately, the increased visibility of transgender activists has not led to universal acceptance. As transgender activists gain a wider audience, people are increasingly open to analyzing this issue and looking at it from different points of view.

CHAPTER 1

WHAT THE EXPERTS SAY

All throughout human history, there have been individuals who have not fit into the strict concept of a gender binary that assumes only male and female gender identity. Although the question of gender identity is not a new phenomenon, it is a complex issue, and experts are still trying to figure out the reasons why some people are transgender. As a consequence, there is controversy about the treatment of people diagnosed with gender dysphoria, and in fact some people believe that this should not be a diagnosis at all. Gender dysphoria is a medical diagnosis used not to identify the condition as a mental disorder but rather to treat the feelings of stress and depression that can go along with it. In one selection in this chapter, Richard A. Friedman, a psychiatrist, examines this clinical diagnosis.

In addition to the psychological considerations of gender identity itself, discrimination against transgender people is another matter with which experts are concerned. Transphobia has a severe negative impact on many people's lives, and many trans people have been killed or seriously injured in transphobic attacks. The remaining selections in this chapter address questions that people may have about gender identity and how to support those who identify as transgender—and remind us that many trans people around the world experience discrimination in their everyday lives.

"ANSWERS TO YOUR QUESTIONS ABOUT TRANSGENDER PEOPLE, GENDER IDENTITY, AND GENDER EXPRESSION," BY THE AMERICAN PSYCHOLOGICAL ASSOCIATION, 2011

WHAT DOES TRANSGENDER MEAN?

Transgender is an umbrella term for persons whose gender identity, gender expression, or behavior does not conform to that typically associated with the sex to which they were assigned at birth. Gender identity refers to a person's internal sense of being male, female, or something else; gender expression refers to the way a person communicates gender identity to others through behavior, clothing, hairstyles, voice, or body characteristics. "Trans" is sometimes used as shorthand for "transgender." While transgender is generally a good term to use, not everyone whose appearance or behavior is gender-nonconforming will identify as a transgender person. The ways in which transgender people are talked about in popular culture, academia, and science are constantly changing, particularly as individuals' awareness, knowledge, and openness about transgender people and their experiences grow.

WHAT IS THE DIFFERENCE BETWEEN SEX AND GENDER?

Sex is assigned at birth, refers to one's biological status as either male or female, and is associated primarily with physical attributes such as chromosomes, hormone prevalence, and external and internal anatomy. Gender refers to the socially constructed roles, behaviors, activities, and attributes that a given society considers appropriate for boys and men or girls and women. These influence the ways people act, interact, and feel about themselves. While aspects of biological sex are similar across different cultures, aspects of gender may differ.

Various conditions that lead to atypical development of physical sex characteristics are collectively referred to as intersex conditions. For information about people with intersex conditions (also known as disorders of sex development), see APA's brochure "Answers to Your Questions About Individuals With Intersex Conditions."

HAVE TRANSGENDER PEOPLE ALWAYS EXISTED?

Transgender persons have been documented in many indigenous, Western, and Eastern cultures and societies from antiquity to the present day. However, the meaning of gender nonconformity may vary from culture to culture. What are some categories or types of transgender people? Many identities fall under the transgender umbrella. The term *transsexual* refers to people whose gender identity is different from their assigned sex. Often, transsexual people alter or wish to alter their bodies through hormones, surgery, and other means to make their bodies as congruent as possible with their gender identities. This process of transition through medical intervention is often referred to as sex or gender reassignment, but more recently is also referred to as gender affirmation. People who were assigned female but identify and live as male and alter or wish to alter their bodies through medical intervention to more closely resemble their gender identity are known as transsexual men or transmen (also known as female-to-male or FTM). Conversely, people who were assigned male but identify and live as female and alter or wish to alter their bodies through medical intervention to more closely resemble their gender identity are known as transsexual women or transwomen (also known as male-to-female or MTF). Some individuals who transition from one gender to another prefer to be referred to as a man or a woman rather than as transgender.

People who *cross-dress* wear clothing that is traditionally or stereotypically worn by another gender in their culture. They vary in how completely they cross-dress, from one article of clothing to fully cross-dressing. Those who cross-dress are usually comfortable with their assigned sex and do not wish to change it. Cross-dressing is a form of gender expression and is not necessarily tied to erotic activity. Cross-dressing is not indicative of sexual orientation (see "Answers to Your Questions for a Better Understanding of Sexual Orientation & Homosexuality" for more information on sexual orientation). The degree of societal acceptance for cross-dressing varies for males and females. In some cultures, one gender may be given more latitude than another for wearing clothing associated with a different gender.

The term *drag queens* generally refers to men who dress as women for the purpose of entertaining others at bars, clubs, or other events. The term *drag kings* refers to women who dress as men for the purpose of entertaining others at bars, clubs, or other events.

Genderqueer is a term that some people use who identify their gender as falling outside the binary constructs of "male" and "female." They may define their gender as falling somewhere on a continuum between male and female, or they may define it as wholly different from these terms. They may also request that pronouns be used that are neither masculine nor feminine, such as "zie" instead of "he" or "she," or "hir" instead of "his" or "her." Some genderqueer people do not identify as transgender.

Other categories of transgender people include *androgynous, multigendered, gender nonconforming, third gender,* and *two-spirit* people. Exact definitions of these terms vary from person to person and may change over time but often include a sense of blending or alternating genders. Some people who use these terms to describe themselves see traditional, binary concepts of gender as restrictive.

WHY ARE SOME PEOPLE TRANSGENDER?

There is no single explanation for why some people are transgender. The diversity of transgender expression and experiences argues against any simple or unitary explanation. Many experts believe that biological factors such as genetic influences and prenatal experiences later in adolescence or adulthood may all contribute to the development of transgender identities.

HOW PREVALENT ARE TRANSGENDER PEOPLE?

It is difficult to accurately estimate the number of transgender people, mostly because there are no population studies that accurately and completely account for the range of gender identity and gender expression.

WHAT IS THE RELATIONSHIP BETWEEN GENDER IDENTITY AND SEXUAL ORIENTATION?

Gender identity and sexual orientation are not the same. Sexual orientation refers to an individual's enduring physical, romantic, and/or emotional attraction to another person, whereas gender identity refers to one's internal sense of being male, female, or something else. Transgender people may be straight, lesbian, gay, bisexual, or asexual, just as nontransgender people may be. Some recent research has shown that a change or a new exploration period in partner attraction may occur during the process of transition. However, transgender people usually remain as attached to loved ones after transition as they were before transition. Transgender people usually label their sexual orientation using their gender as a reference. For example, a transgender woman, or a person who is assigned male at birth and transitions to female, who is attracted to other women would be identified as a lesbian or gay woman. Likewise, a transgender man, or a person who is assigned female at birth and transitions to male, who is attracted to other men would be identified as a gay man.

HOW DOES SOMEONE KNOW THAT THEY ARE TRANSGENDER?

Transgender people experience their transgender identity in a variety of ways and may become aware of their transgender identity at any age. Some can trace their transgender identities and feelings back to their earliest memories. They may have vague feelings of "not fitting in" with people of their assigned sex or specific wishes to be something other than their assigned sex. Others become aware of their transgender identities or begin to explore and experience gender-nonconforming attitudes and behaviors during adolescence or much later in life. Some embrace their transgender feelings, while others struggle with feelings of shame or confusion. Those who transition later in life may have struggled to fit in adequately as their assigned sex only to later face dissatisfaction with their lives. Some transgender people, transsexuals in particular, experience intense dissatisfaction with their sex assigned at birth, physical sex characteristics, or the gender role associated with that sex. These individuals often seek gender-affirming treatments.

WHAT SHOULD PARENTS DO IF THEIR CHILD APPEARS TO BE TRANSGENDER OR GENDER NONCONFORMING?

Parents may be concerned about a child who appears to be gender-nonconforming for a variety of reasons. Some children express a great deal of distress about their assigned sex at birth or the gender roles they are expected to follow. Some children experience difficult social interactions with peers and adults because of their gender expression. Parents may become concerned when what they believed to be a "phase" does not pass. Parents of gender-nonconforming children may need to work with schools and other institutions to address their children's particular needs and ensure their children's safety. It is helpful to consult with mental health and medical professionals familiar with gender issues in children to decide how to best address these concerns. It is not helpful to force the child to act in a more gender-conforming way. Peer support from other parents of gender-nonconforming children may also be helpful.

HOW DO TRANSSEXUALS MAKE A GENDER TRANSITION?

Transitioning from one gender to another is a complex process and may involve transition to a gender that is neither traditionally male nor female. People who transition often start by expressing their preferred gender in situations where they feel safe. They typically work up to living full time as members of their preferred gender by making many changes a little at a time. While there is no "right" way to transition genders, there are some common social changes transgender people experience that may involve one or more of the following: adopting the appearance of the desired sex through changes in clothing and grooming, adopting a new name, changing sex designation on identity documents (if possible), using hormone therapy treatment, and/or undergoing medical procedures that modify their body to conform with their gender identity.

Every transgender person's process or transition differs. Because of this, many factors may determine how the individual wishes to live and express their gender identity. Finding a qualified mental health professional who is experienced in providing affirmative care for transgender people is an important first step. A qualified professional can provide guidance and referrals to other helping professionals. Connecting with other transgender people through peer support groups and transgender community organizations is also helpful.

The World Professional Association for Transgender Health (WPATH), a professional organization devoted to the treatment of transgender people, publishes *The Standards of Care for Gender Identity Disorders*, which offers recommendations for the provision of gender affirmation procedures and services.

IS BEING TRANSGENDER A MENTAL DISORDER?

A psychological state is considered a mental disorder only if it causes significant distress or disability. Many transgender people do not experience their gender as distressing or disabling, which implies that identifying as transgender does not constitute a mental disorder. For these individuals, the significant problem is finding affordable resources, such as counseling, hormone therapy, medical procedures, and the social support necessary to freely express their gender identity and minimize discrimination. Many other obstacles may lead to distress, including a lack of acceptance within society, direct or indirect experiences with discrimination, or assault. These experiences may lead many transgender people to suffer with anxiety, depression, or related disorders at higher rates than nontransgender persons.

According to the *Diagnostic and Statistical Manual of Mental Disorders (DSM-5),* people who experience intense, persistent gender incongruence can be given the diagnosis of "gender dysphoria." Some contend that the diagnosis inappropriately pathologizes gender noncongruence and should be eliminated. Others argue it is essential to retain the diagnosis to ensure access to care. The *International Classification of Diseases (ICD)* is under revision, and there may be changes to its current classification of intense persistent gender incongruence as "gender identity disorder."

WHAT KINDS OF DISCRIMINATION DO TRANSGENDER PEOPLE FACE?

Anti-discrimination laws in most U.S. cities and states do not protect transgender people from discrimination based on gender identity or gender expression. Consequently, transgender people in most cities and states face discrimination in nearly every aspect of their lives. The National Center for Transgender Equality and the National Gay and Lesbian Task Force released a report in 2011 entitled "Injustice at Every Turn," which confirmed the pervasive and severe discrimination faced by transgender people. Out of a sample of nearly 6,500 transgender people, the report found that transgender people experience high levels of discrimination in employment, housing, health care, education, legal systems, and even in their families. (Editor's note: the report can be found at http://endtransdiscrimination.org.)

Transgender people may also have additional identities that may affect the types of discrimination they experience. Groups with such additional identities include transgender people of racial, ethnic, or religious minority backgrounds; transgender people of lower socioeconomic statuses; transgender people with disabilities; transgender youth; transgender elderly; and others. Experiencing discrimination may cause significant psychological stress, often leaving transgender individuals to wonder whether they were discriminated against because of their gender identity or gender expression, another sociocultural identity, or some combination of all of these.

According to the study, while discrimination is pervasive for the majority of transgender people, the inter-section of anti-transgender bias and persistent, structural racism is especially severe. People of color in general fare worse than White transgender people, with African American transgender individuals faring far worse than all other transgender populations examined.

Many transgender people are the targets of hate crimes. They are also the victims of subtle discrimina-tion—which includes everything from glances or glares of disapproval or discomfort to invasive questions about their body parts.

HOW CAN I BE SUPPORTIVE OF TRANSGENDER FAMILY MEMBERS, FRIENDS, OR SIGNIFICANT OTHERS?

- Educate yourself about transgender issues by read-ing books, attending conferences, and consulting with transgender experts. Be aware of your attitudes con-cerning people with gender-nonconforming appear-ance or behavior.
- Know that transgender people have membership in various sociocultural identity groups (e.g., race, social class, religion, age, disability, etc.) and there is not one universal way to look or be transgender.
- Use names and pronouns that are appropriate to the per-son's gender presentation and identity; if in doubt, ask.

- Don't make assumptions about transgender people's sexual orientation, desire for hormonal or medical treatment, or other aspects of their identity or transition plans. If you have a reason to know (e.g., you are a physician conducting a necessary physical exam or you are a person who is interested in dating someone you've learned is transgender), ask.
- Don't confuse gender nonconformity with being transgender. Not all people who appear androgynous or gender nonconforming identify as transgender or desire gender affirmation treatment.
- Keep the lines of communication open with the transgender person in your life.
- Get support in processing your own reactions. It can take some time to adjust to seeing someone you know well transitioning. Having someone close to you transition will be an adjustment and can be challenging, especially for partners, parents, and children.
- Seek support in dealing with your feelings. You are not alone. Mental health professionals and support groups for family, friends, and significant others of transgender people can be useful resources.
- Advocate for transgender rights, including social and economic justice and appropriate psychological care. Familiarize yourself with the local and state or provincial laws that protect transgender people from discrimination.

Copyright © 2011 American Psychological Association. Updated in 2014.

1. In your opinion, do you think being transgender should be classified as a mental disorder?

"HOW CHANGEABLE IS GENDER?," BY RICHARD A. FRIEDMAN, FROM THE *NEW YORK TIMES*, AUGUST 22, 2015

THANKS to Caitlyn Jenner, and the military's changing policies, transgender people are gaining acceptance—and living in a bigger, more understanding spotlight than at any previous time.

We're learning to be more accepting of transgender individuals. And we're learning more about gender identity, too.

The prevailing narrative seems to be that gender is a social construct and that people can move between genders to arrive at their true identity.

But if gender were nothing more than a social convention, why was it necessary for Caitlyn Jenner to undergo facial surgeries, take hormones and remove her body hair? The fact that some transgender individuals use hormone treatment and surgery to switch gender speaks to the inescapable biology at the heart of gender identity.

This is not to suggest that gender identity is simply binary—male or female—or that gender identity is inflexible for everyone. Nor does it mean that conventional gender roles always feel right; the sheer number of people who experience varying degrees of mismatch between their preferred gender and their body makes this very clear.

In fact, recent neuroscience research suggests that gender identity may exist on a spectrum and that gender dysphoria fits well within the range of human biological variation. For example, Georg S. Kranz at the Medical

University of Vienna and colleagues elsewhere reported in a 2014 study in *The Journal of Neuroscience* that individuals who identified as transsexuals—those who wanted sex reassignment—had structural differences in their brains that were between their desired gender and their genetic sex.

Dr. Kranz studied four different groups: female-to-male transsexuals; male-to-female transsexuals; and controls who were born female or male and identify as such. Since hormones can have a direct effect on the brain, both transsexual groups were studied before they took any sex hormones, so observed differences in brain function and structure would not be affected by the treatment. He used a high-resolution technique called diffusion tensor imaging, a special type of M.R.I., to examine the white matter microstructure of subjects' brains.

What Dr. Kranz found was intriguing: In several brain regions, people born female with a female gender identity had the highest level of something called mean diffusivity, followed by female-to-male transsexuals. Next came male-to-female transsexuals, and then the males with a male gender identity, who had the lowest levels.

In other words, it seems that Dr. Kranz may have found a neural signature of the transgender experience: a mismatch between one's gender identity and physical sex. Transgender people have a brain that is structurally different than the brain of a nontransgender male or female—someplace in between men and women.

This gradient of structural brain differences, from females to males, with transgender people in between, suggests that gender identity has a neural basis and that it exists on a spectrum, like so much of human behavior.

Some theorize that the transgender experience might arise, in part, from a quirk of brain development. It turns out that the sexual differentiation of the brain happens during the second half of pregnancy, later than sexual differentiation of the genitals and body, which begins during the first two months of pregnancy. And since these two processes can be influenced independently of each other, it may be possible to have a mismatch between gender-specific brain development and that of the body.

Is it really so surprising that gender identity might, like sexual orientation, be on a spectrum? After all, one can be exclusively straight or exclusively gay—or anything in between. But variability in a behavior shouldn't be confused with its malleability. There is little evidence, for example, that you really can change your sexual orientation. Sure, you can change your sexual behavior, but your inner sexual fantasies endure.

In fact, attempts to change a person's sexual orientation, through so-called reparative therapy, have been debunked as quackery and rightly condemned by the psychiatric profession as potentially harmful.

Of course, people should have the freedom to assume whatever gender role makes them comfortable and refer to themselves with whatever pronoun they choose; we should encourage people to be who they really feel they are, not who or what society would like them to be. I wonder, if we were a more tolerant society that welcomed all types of gender identity, what the impact might be on gender dysphoria. How many transgender individuals would feel the need to physically change gender, if they truly felt accepted with whatever gender role they choose?

At the same time, we have to acknowledge that gender identity is a complex phenomenon, involving a mix of genes, hormones and social influence. And there is no getting around the fact that biology places constraints on our capacity to reimagine ourselves and to change, and it's important to understand those limitations.

The critical question is not whether there is a range of gender identity—it seems clear that there is. Rather, it is to what extent and in which populations gender identity is malleable, and to what extent various strategies to change one's body and behavior to match a preferred gender will give people the psychological satisfaction they seek.

Although transsexualism (defined as those who want to change or do change their body) is very rare—a recent meta-analysis estimated the prevalence at about 5 per 100,000—it garners much media attention. What do we really know about how these individuals feel and function in their new role?

The data are all over the map. One meta-analysis published in 2010 of follow-up studies suggested that about 80 percent of transgender individuals reported subjective improvement in terms of gender dysphoria and quality of life. But the review emphasized that many of the studies were suboptimal: All of them were observational and most lacked controls.

Dr. Cecilia Dhejne and colleagues at the Karolinska Institute in Sweden have done one of the largest follow-up studies of transsexuals, published in *PLOS One* in 2011. They compared a group of 324 Swedish transsexuals for an average of more than 10 years after gender reassignment with controls and found that transsexuals had 19 times the rate of suicide and about three times the mortality rate compared with controls. When the researchers controlled for baseline rates of depression and suicide, which are known to be higher in transsexuals, they still found elevated rates of depression and suicide after sex reassignment.

This study doesn't prove that gender reassignment per se was the cause of the excess morbidity and mortality in transsexual people; to answer that, you would have to compare transgender people who were randomly assigned to reassignment to those who were not. Still, even if hormone replacement and surgery relieve gender dysphoria, the overall outcome with gender reassignment doesn't look so good—a fact that only underscores the need for better medical treatments in general for transgender individuals and better psychiatric care after reassignment.

Alarmingly, 41 percent of transgender and gender nonconforming individuals attempt suicide at some point in their lifetime compared with 4.6 percent of the general public, according to a joint study by the American Foundation for Suicide Prevention and the Williams Institute. The disturbingly high rate of suicide attempts among transgender people likely reflects a complex interaction of mental health factors and experiences of harassment, discrimination and violence. The study analyzed data from the National Transgender Discrimination Survey, which documents the bullying, harassment, rejection by family and other assorted horrors.

On a broader level, the outcome studies suggest that gender reassignment doesn't necessarily give everyone what they really want or make them happier.

Nowhere is this issue more contentious than in children and adolescents who experience gender dysphoria or the sense that their desired gender mismatches their body. In fact, there are few areas of medicine or psychiatry where the debate has become so heated. I was surprised to discover how many professional colleagues in this area either warned me to be careful about what I wrote or were reluctant to talk with me on the record for fear of reprisal from the transgender community.

If gender identity were a fixed and stable phenomenon in all young people, there would be little to argue about. But we have learned over the past two decades that, like so much else in child and adolescent behavior, the experience of gender dysphoria is itself often characterized by flux.

Several studies have tracked the persistence of gender dysphoria in children as they grow. For example, Dr. Richard Green's study of young boys with gender dysphoria in the 1980s found that only one of the 44 boys was gender dysphoric by adolescence or adulthood. And a 2008 study by Madeleine S. C. Wallein, at the VU University Medical Center in the Netherlands, reported that in a group of 77 young people, ages 5 to 12, who all had gender dysphoria at the start of the study, 70 percent of the boys and 36 percent of the girls were no longer gender dysphoric after an average of 10 years' follow-up.

THIS strongly suggests that gender dysphoria in young children is highly unstable and likely to change. Whether the loss of gender dysphoria is spontaneous or the result of parental or social influence is anyone's guess. Moreover, we can't predict reliably which gender dysphoric children will be "persisters" and which will be "desisters."

So if you were a parent of, say, an 8-year-old boy who said he really wanted to be a girl, you might not immediately accede to your child's wish, knowing that there is a high probability—80 percent, in some studies—that that desire will disappear with time.

The counterargument is that to delay treatment is to consign this child to psychological suffering of potentially unknown duration. This is a disturbing possibility, though much can be done to help alleviate depression or anxiety without necessarily embarking on gender change. But rather than managing these psychological symptoms and watchfully waiting, some groups recommend pharmacologically delaying the onset of puberty in gender dysphoric children until age 16, before proceeding to reassignment. Puberty suppression is presumed reversible, and can be stopped if the adolescent's gender dysphoria desists. But the risks of this treatment are not fully understood. Even more troubling, some doctors appear to be starting reassignment earlier. Some argue that the medical and psychiatric professions have a responsibility to respond to the child as he or she really is.

But if anything marks what a child really is, it is experimentation and flux. Why, then, would one subject a child to hormones and gender reassignment if there is a high likelihood that the gender dysphoria will resolve?

With adolescents, the story is very different: About three quarters of gender dysphoric teens may be "persisters," which makes decisions about gender reassignment at this age more secure.

Clinicians who take an agnostic watch-and-wait approach in children with gender dysphoria have been accused by some in the transgender community of imposing societal values—that boys should remain boys and girls remain girls—on their patients and have compared them to clinicians who practice reparative therapy for gays.

I think that criticism is misguided. First, there is abundant evidence that reparative therapy is both ineffective and often harmful, while there is no comparable data in the area of gender dysphoria. Second, unlike sexual orientation, which tends to be stable, gender dysphoria in many young people clearly isn't. Finally, when it comes to gender dysphoria, the evidence for therapeutics are simply poor to start with: There are no randomized clinical trials and very few comparative studies examining different approaches for this population.

Given the absence of good treatment-outcome data, how can anyone—whether transgender activist, parent or clinician—be sure of the best course of action?

There is obviously a huge gap between rapidly shifting cultural attitudes about gender identity and our scientific understanding of them. Until we have better data, what's wrong with a little skepticism? After all, medical and psychological treatments should be driven by the best available scientific evidence—not political pressure or cherished beliefs.

1. Do you think that a differing brain structure is what makes people transgender, as scientists featured in this article argue?

2. The author asks: "How many transgender individuals would feel the need to physically change gender if they truly felt accepted with whatever gender role they choose?" What do you think?

EXCERPTS FROM "A PRACTITIONER'S RESOURCE GUIDE: HELPING FAMILIES TO SUPPORT THEIR LGBT CHILDREN," FROM THE SUBSTANCE ABUSE AND MENTAL HEALTH SERVICES ADMINISTRATION, 2014

INTRODUCTION

Since the early 1990s, young people have increasingly been coming out or identifying as lesbian, gay, and bisexual, and more recently as transgender, during adolescence. This coincides with greater awareness and visibility of lesbian, gay, bisexual, and transgender (LGBT) people in society, the media, schools, congregations, and communities. More widespread access to information about sexual orientation, gender identity, and LGBT resources through the internet has contributed to significant changes in how children and adolescents learn about LGBT people and their lives. And increasingly, this has helped young people come out at much earlier ages than prior generations of LGBT adults.

Coming out at earlier ages has important implications for how practitioners work with children, youth, and families, how they educate parents, families, and caregivers about sexual orientation and gender identity, and how services are provided to LGBT children and adolescents. Historically, services for LGB youth and later for transgender youth were developed to protect them from harm, including from parents and families that were perceived as rejecting or incapable of supporting their sexual minority children. As a result, services evolved over several decades to serve LGBT adolescents either individually—like adults—or through peer support, and not in the context of their families (Ryan, 2004; Ryan & Chen-Hayes, 2013).

Even though families, in general, play a critical role in child and adolescent development and well-being, and connections to family are protective against major health risks (Resnick et al., 1997), until recently little was known about how parents reacted to their LGBT children from the perspective of parents and caregivers (Bouris et al., 2010; Diamond et al., 2012; Ryan, 2010) or how they adapted and adjusted to their LGBT children over time. As a result, many practitioners assumed that little could be done to help parents and families who were perceived as rejecting to support their LGBT children. So few practitioners tried to engage or work with these families (Ryan & Chen-Hayes, 2013). Nevertheless, earlier ages of coming out coupled with emerging research which indicates that families of LGBT adolescents contribute significantly to their children's health and wellbeing call for a paradigm shift in how services and care are provided for LGBT children and adolescents (Ryan, 2010).

This new family-oriented approach to services and care requires practitioners to proactively engage and work with families with LGBT children and adolescents. This includes providing accurate information on sexual orientation and gender identity for parents and caregivers early in their child's development; engaging, educating, counseling, and making appropriate referrals for families with LGBT children; and in particular, helping parents and caregivers who react to their LGBT children with ambivalence and rejection understand how their reactions contribute to health risks for their LGBT children (Ryan & Chen-Hayes, 2013).

The overall objective in helping families learn to support their LGBT children is not to change their values or deeply-held beliefs. Instead, practitioners should aim to meet parents, families, and caregivers "where they are," to build an alliance to support their LGBT children, and to help them understand that family reactions that are experienced as rejection by their LGBT child contribute to serious health concerns and inhibit their child's development and wellbeing (Ryan & Diaz, 2011; Ryan & Chen-Hayes, 2013)

EARLIER AGES OF AWARENESS & COMING OUT

A seminal study of LGB identity and adolescent development found that young people report having their first "crush" or attraction for another person, on average, at around age 10 (Herdt & Boxer, 1993). Subsequent studies on LGB youth have reported comparable ages of first awareness of sexual attraction (e.g., D'Augelli, 2006; Rosario, Schrimshaw, & Hunter, 2009), and coming out at much younger ages than prior generations of LGB adults. Among contemporary youth, researchers from the Family Acceptance Project found that adolescents self-identified as LGB, on average, at age 13.4. And increasingly, parents and families report children identifying as gay at earlier ages—between ages 7 and 12.

Practitioners who work with transgender and gender nonconforming children and youth note that gender identity is expressed at early ages (Brill & Pepper, 2008), most often by age 3 (Leibowitz & Spack, 2011). As with LGB adolescents, the internet and media have significantly increased awareness of gender diversity and of the needs and experiences of transgender and gender non-conforming children, adolescents and adults. Because children can express a clear sense of gender identity at very early ages, many are able to communicate their experiences to parents and caregivers, so there is greater awareness among some families that a child or adolescent might be transgender. As a result, more parents are seeking accurate information about gender development and local sources of support.

Still, many families have strict cultural expectations about gender role behavior for males and females and have great difficulty tolerating gender non-conforming behavior in their children and adolescents (e.g., Malpas, 2011). This includes children and youth who are lesbian, gay, and bisexual, as well as heterosexual. A significant number of families have never heard of the word *transgender* and have little understanding of the distress that children who are gender non-conforming may experience on a daily basis. This may include parents and families who have less access to accurate information, based on sociocultural and linguistic backgrounds and/or geographic location.

These early ages of self-awareness and coming out as LGBT during childhood and adolescence call for practitioners to expand their approach to care from serving LGBT young people either alone as individuals or through peer support to providing services and support in the context of their families and caregivers (Ryan & Chen-Hayes, 2013). This need is heightened by the lack of available services and trained practitioners to provide family-oriented services and support for LGBT children and adolescents across practice disciplines and care settings.

Before research was conducted that included LGBT adolescents, parents, foster parents, and other key family members, perceptions of how parents and families would react to their LGBT children were pre-dominantly negative (Ryan, 2010). However, an in-depth study of LGBT adolescents and families found that family reactions to their LGBT children were much more varied and hopeful than had been previously assumed (Ryan, 2004; Ryan & Chen-Hayes, 2013). This study found that:

Family reactions to their LGBT adolescents range from highly rejecting to highly accepting. Thus, a proportion of families respond with acceptance, and more with ambivalence, to learning about their child's LGBT identity—and not with uniform rejection as had been previously assumed.

Rejecting families become less rejecting over time, and access to accurate information is a critical factor in helping parents, families, and caregivers learn to support their LGBT children.

Parents and families want to help their LGBT children and to keep their families together, but many do not know how.

Parents and caregivers who are perceived as rejecting their LGBT children and who engage in rejecting behaviors (e.g., trying to change their child's sexual orientation and gender expression) are motivated by care and concern for their LGBT children—and by trying to help their LGBT child "fit in," have a "good life," and be accepted by others.

Negative outcomes for many LGBT youth, including suicide, homelessness, and placement in foster care or juvenile justice facilities, can be prevented or reduced if parents, families, and caregivers can turn to a knowledgeable source for guidance, accurate information, and support.

Many parents and families whose children end up out of home (e.g., homeless or in custodial care) want to re-connect and to have an ongoing relationship with their LGBT children despite assumptions by others that they do not want to have any involvement with their LGBT children's lives.

RELATIONSHIP TO RISK & WELL-BEING

Research has also found that parents and caregivers play a critical role in their LGBT children's health and well-being (e.g., Ryan et al., 2009; Ryan et al., 2010). In particular, families help protect against suicidal behaviors (Eisenberg & Resnick, 2006; Mustanski & Liu, 2013; Ryan et al., 2010). Research with LGBT youth and families, foster families, and caregivers has identified more than 100 specific ways that parents and caregivers express acceptance and rejection of their LGBT children (Ryan, 2009; Ryan, 2010). This includes behaviors such as preventing LGBT youth from learning about their LGBT identity versus connecting them with a positive role model to show them options for the future (see Ryan, 2009). These family reactions were then measured in a follow up study of LGBT young adults to assess the relationship of family acceptance and rejection during adolescence to health and mental health in young adulthood.

This research found what many providers have known intuitively for years: that LGBT young people whose parents and caregivers reject them report high levels of negative health problems (Ryan et al., 2009), and those whose parents support them show greater well-being, better general health, and significantly decreased risk for suicide, depression, and substance abuse (Ryan et al., 2010). Additional research from this project provides key information on school-based and faith-based experiences, including the relationship between condemnation, victimization, and support of LGBT adolescents and their health and well-being in young adulthood.

INCREASING FAMILY SUPPORT

Working closely with many racially and ethnically diverse families, LGBT youth, and young adults in applying this research showed that families—even those who were very rejecting—could learn to modify rejecting behavior and increase support for their LGBT children. This requires practitioners to provide education, guidance, and support in ways that resonate for them (Ryan, 2010). Several years of intervention and resource development work has led to the generation of a series of multicultural family education materials; research-based family intervention videos; assessment tools; and intervention strategies to help diverse families support their LGBT children.

Grounded in a strengths-based perspective, this family intervention framework (Ryan & Chen-Hayes, 2013; Ryan & Diaz, 2011) views families and caregivers as potential allies in reducing risk, promoting well-being, and creating a healthy future for their LGBT children. This approach views the family's cultural values—including deeply-held beliefs—as strengths. Research findings are aligned with underlying values to help families understand that it is specific behaviors and communication patterns that contribute to both their LGBT child's risk and their well-being.

HELPING FAMILIES DECREASE RISK & INCREASE WELL-BEING FOR THEIR LGBT CHILDREN

Beyond building an alliance and showing families that a practitioner respects their values and beliefs, the primary mechanism for change is helping families understand that there is a powerful relationship between their words, actions, and behaviors and their LGBT child's risk and well-being. Parental and caregiver reactions to an LGBT child or adolescent also affect their whole family.

Families respond to their LGBT children based on what they know, what they hear from their family, clergy, close friends, and information sources, including providers who may also have misinformation about sexual orientation and gender identity, especially in childhood and adolescence. As a result, parents and families who believe that homosexuality and gender non-conformity are wrong or are harmful for their LGBT children may respond in a variety of ways to try to prevent their children from becoming gay or transgender.

This may include: preventing their child from having an LGBT friend, learning about their LGBT identity, or participating in a support group for LGBT youth (such as a Gay Straight Alliance or school diversity club), or excluding their child from family events and activities. Families and caregivers who respond in these ways do so without understanding that these reactions are experienced as rejection by their LGBT children and that they are significantly related to attempted suicide and other serious health concerns for LGBT young people (e.g., Ryan, 2009).

Parents and families who engage in these behaviors are typically motivated by helping their children and protecting them from harm. In this case, families are trying to prevent their children from adopting what they perceive as a "lifestyle" or "choice" that they believe will hurt them. Understanding that specific reactions that parents and families think are caring but that LGBT youth experience as rejecting and harmful—and that contribute to serious health problems—helps motivate parents, families, and caregivers to modify and stop rejecting behaviors, to support LGBT children (Ryan, 2009; Ryan & Diaz, 2011).

1. This resource guide is written for licensed health practitioners who want to help families support their LGBT (lesbian, gay, bisexual, or transgender) children. How important do you think family support is to gender non-conforming individuals?

2. What do you think about the belief, as stated in this resource guide, that families who show "rejecting behaviors" to their LGBT children are actually trying to help and protect their children?

CHAPTER 2

WHAT THE GOVERNMENT AND CHURCH LEADERS SAY

O ne of the main purposes of governments is to protect their citizens and, considering transgender individuals frequently suffer from discrimination, it would seem that governments have their work cut out for them. In recent years, many governments in the Western world have taken steps to counteract discrimination against transgender people and uphold their human rights, but reality shows that they are still far from reaching their goal. This chapter includes governmental documents from both the Europe Commissioner for Human Rights and the United States Office of Personnel Management, Equal Employment Opportunity Commission, Office of Special Counsel, and Merit Systems Protection Board that show how Western governments are addressing discrimination against transgender people.

But it's not only those in secular and democratically elected positions who must grapple with issues of gender identity. Faith-based leaders also have to decide how their religious communities will respond if some of their members do not conform to their traditional concept of gender. Two selections included in this chapter highlight Catholic responses to the transgender community in order to address this important issue.

EXCERPT FROM "HUMAN RIGHTS AND GENDER IDENTITY," BY THOMAS HAMMARBERG, COUNCIL OF EUROPE COMMISSIONER FOR HUMAN RIGHTS, THE COUNCIL OF EUROPE, JULY 29, 2009

I. INTRODUCTION

Gender identity is one of the most fundamental aspects of life. The sex of a person is usually assigned at birth and becomes a social and legal fact from there on. However, a relatively small number of people experience problems with being a member of the sex recorded at birth. This can also be so for intersex persons whose bodies incorporate both or certain aspects of both male and female physiology, and at times their genital anatomy. For others, problems arise because their innate perception of themselves is not in conformity with the sex assigned to them at birth. These persons are referred to as 'transgender' or 'transsexual' persons, and the current paper relates to this group of people.

The human rights situation of transgender persons has long been ignored and neglected, although the problems they face are serious and often specific to this group alone. Transgender people experience a high degree of discrimination, intolerance and outright violence. Their basic human rights are violated, including the right to life, the right to physical integrity and the right to health.

Although the number of transgender persons is small, it should be pointed out that the transgender community is very diverse. It includes pre-operative and post-operative transsexual persons, but also persons who do not choose to undergo or do not have access to operations. They may identify as female-to-male (FTM) or male-to-female (MTF) transgender persons, and may or may not have undergone surgery or hormonal therapy. The community also includes cross-dressers, transvestites and other people who do not fit the narrow categories of 'male' or 'female'. Many legal frameworks only seem to refer to transsexual persons, leaving out a decisive part of the community.

In order to understand the concept of gender identity, it is important to distinguish between the notions of 'sex' and 'gender'. While 'sex' primarily refers to the biological difference between women and men, 'gender' also includes the social aspect of the difference between genders in addition to the biological element.

The notion of 'gender identity' offers the opportunity to understand that the sex assigned to an infant at birth might not correspond with the innate gender identity the child develops when he or she grows up. It refers to each person's deeply felt internal and individual experience of gender, which may or may not correspond with the sex assigned at birth, and includes the personal sense of the body and other expressions of gender (i.e. 'gender expression') such as dress, speech and mannerisms. (1) Most people legally defined as man or woman will correspondingly have a male or female gender identity. Transgender persons, however, do not develop that corresponding gender identity and may wish to change their legal, social, and physical status – or parts thereof - to correspond with their gender identity. Modification of bodily appearance or function by dress, medical, surgical or other means is often part of the personal experience of gender by transgender people.

Both the notion of gender identity and the forms of gender expression used in everyday life are important elements for understanding the human rights problems faced by transgender persons. Some legal frameworks in Council of Europe member states, unfortunately, categorise gender identity under 'sexual orientation', which is not accurate since gender identity and sexual orientation are two different concepts. Sexual orientation should be understood as each person's capacity for profound emotional, affectional and sexual attraction to, and intimate and sexual relations with, individuals of a different gender or the same gender or more than one gender (heterosexuality, homosexuality and bisexuality). (2) In addition, many international and national medical classifications impose the diagnosis of mental disorder on transgender persons. Such a diagnosis may become an obstacle to the full enjoyment of human rights by transgender people especially when it is applied in a way to restrict the legal capacity or choice for medical treatment.

The challenge of protecting the human rights of everyone is to apply a consistent human rights approach and not to exclude any group of people. It is clear that many transgender persons do not fully enjoy their fundamental rights both at the level of legal guarantees and that of everyday life. Therefore, there is a need to take a closer look at their situation. This Issue Paper is intended to continue the debate on transgender human rights issues and make the problems encountered by transgender people known more widely. (3) The paper outlines the international human rights framework that should be applied to protect the rights of transgender persons. In the following section, it describes the key human rights concerns regarding transgender persons, including discrimination, intolerance and violence experienced by them. The paper concludes with examples of good practice and a set of recommendations to member states of the Council of Europe.

One obstacle in the drafting of this paper was the lack of data, research and reports on the theme. The limited information available often refers to countries that are member states of the European Union. The lack of data on other countries demonstrates the need for further research and information gathering. The Office of the Commissioner for Human Rights has therefore launched a comparative study on the situation concerning homophobia, transphobia and discrimination on grounds of sexual orientation and gender identity in all Council of Europe member states, including those countries which are not members of the European Union. Nevertheless, the currently available research already points at a bleak situation and calls for urgent measures to be taken to address the concerns identified.

II. INTERNATIONAL HUMAN RIGHTS LAW

In principle, international human rights instruments protect everybody without discrimination. Despite the fact
that gender identity as a discrimination ground, along
with sexual orientation, is often not explicitly mentioned
in international human rights treaties, these treaties do
apply to all persons through their open-ended discrimination clauses. As for the UN Covenant on Economic, Social
and Cultural Rights, this was recently confirmed by the UN
Committee on Economic, Social and Cultural Rights which
stated that "gender identity is recognized as among the
prohibited grounds of discrimination; for example, persons who are transgender, transsexual or intersex often
face serious human rights violations, such as harassment
in schools or in the work place". (4) The European Court of
Human Rights (ECtHR) has applied the European Convention on Human Rights in significant judgments ruling that
states should provide transgender persons the possibility
to undergo surgery leading to full gender reassignment
and that this surgery should be covered by insurance
plans as "medically necessary" treatment. (5) The Court
has also ruled that states should recognise the change of
sex in identity documents. (6)

　　　Other instruments, such as the EU Directives implementing the principle of equal treatment between men
and women in the access to and supply of goods and
services, have closed lists of discrimination grounds and
do not include gender identity specifically. (7) However, the
European Court of Justice (ECJ) has explicitly ruled that
"discrimination arising (…) from the gender reassignment

of the person" is considered as discrimination on the ground of sex in the watershed case *P v S and Cornwall County Council*. This has been confirmed and extended in later case law of the ECJ. (8)

As the specific wording of the ECJ judgment shows, 'sex discrimination' is, however, restricted to transgender persons 'intending to undergo, undergoing or having undergone gender reassigment' whose sex change should be legally recognised by states as a result of rulings by the European Court of Human Rights. (9) 'Sex discrimination' does not cover non-operative transgender people. The latter group may not undergo gender reassignment because of their free choice, their health needs, or the denial of access to any treatment, which is common in many Council of Europe member states. (10) A recent report of the European Union Agency for Fundamental Rights (FRA) states in this regard: "there is no reason not to extend the protection from discrimination beyond these persons, to cover 'cross dressers, and transvestites, people who live permanently in the gender 'opposite' to that on their birth certificate without any medical intervention and all those people who simply wish to present their gender differently". (11) In order to overcome this limitation in coverage of all transgender persons, there is an opportunity to include 'gender identity' explicitly as a discrimination ground in future EU Directives through the review of the EU Gender Directives in 2010. (12)

The recognition of gender identity as one of the universally protected discrimination grounds has also been voiced by the UN High Commissioner for Human Rights: "Neither the existence of national laws, nor the prevalence of custom can ever justify the abuse, attacks, torture and indeed killings that gay, lesbian, bisexual, and transgender persons are subjected to because of who they are or are perceived to be. Because of the stigma attached to issues surrounding sexual orientation and gender identity, violence against LGBT persons is frequently unreported, undocumented and goes ultimately unpunished. Rarely does it provoke public debate and outrage. This shameful silence is the ultimate rejection of the fundamental principle of universality of rights". (13)

UN Special Procedures and treaty bodies have also applied this approach in their work. The UN Special Rapporteur on extrajudicial, summary or arbitrary executions has highlighted several cases of killings of transgender persons and the Special Rapporteur on torture has reported serious abuses against transgender individuals in various country reports. The UN Committee against Torture has specifically addressed the issue of abuses against transgender activists. Moreover, the UN High Commissioner for Refugees has addressed problems transgender persons encounter when applying for asylum or being recognised as a refugee, for example on occasions where a transgender individual is asked by the authorities to produce identity documents and his or her physical appearance does not correspond to the sex indicated in the documents. (14)

The Parliamentary Assembly of the Council of Europe adopted a *Recommendation on the Condition of Transsexuals* in 1989. (15) Currently a report is under preparation within the Assembly's Committee on Legal Affairs and Human Rights which will cover, inter alia, discrimination based on gender identity. The Committee of Ministers of the Council of Europe has in several replies to questions from members of the Parliamentary Assembly recalled the principle of equal enjoyment of human rights regardless of any grounds such as gender identity. Furthermore, on 2 July 2008, the Committee of Ministers decided to step up action to combat discrimination on grounds of sexual orientation and gender identity. This resulted in the setting up of an intergovernmental Expert Group, which has been tasked to prepare a Recommendation for the 47 Council of Europe member states. The European Parliament issued a *Resolution on Discrimination Against Transsexuals* in 1989. (16) The Resolution calls on EU Member States to take steps for the protection of transsexual persons and to pass legislation to further this end. In more general Resolutions in 2006 and 2007, the situation of transgender persons has also been paid attention to by the European Parliament. (17)

In a large scale international effort to promote international standards on sexual orientation and gender identity, a group of distinguished experts in international human rights law published in 2007 the *Yogyakarta Principles on the Application of Human Rights Law in Relation to Sexual Orientation and Gender Identity*. While not adopted as an international standard, the principles are already cited by UN bodies, national courts, and many governments have made them a guiding tool for defining their policies in the matter. The Commissioner for Human Rights has endorsed the *Yogyakarta Principles* and considers them as an important tool for identifying the obligations of states to respect, protect and fulfill the human rights of all persons, regardless of their gender identity.

Of particular relevance is Yogyakarta Principle number 3: 'Everyone has the right to recognition everywhere as a person before the law. Persons of diverse sexual orientations and gender identities shall enjoy legal capacity in all aspects of life. Each person's self-defined sexual orientation and gender identity is integral to their personality and is one of the most basic aspects of self-determination, dignity and freedom. No one shall be forced to undergo medical procedures, including sex reassignment surgery, sterilisation or hormonal therapy, as a requirement for legal recognition of their gender identity. No status, such as marriage or parenthood, may be invoked as such to prevent the legal recognition of a person's gender identity. No one shall be subjected to pressure to conceal, suppress or deny their sexual orientation or gender identity". (18)

IV. GOOD PRACTICES

The human rights situation of transgender people in Europe is not positive. However, some of the problems have been acknowledged and 'good practices' are increasing. In the legal field we have recently seen constitutional courts acknowledging that national laws violate the human rights of transgender persons. In the UK the Gender Recognition Bill can, to a large extent, and excepting the divorce requirement, be considered an example of good practice. It was drafted with the participation of transgender people and led to a viable format, circumventing violations like forced sterilisation, medical treatment conditions, or exaggerated procedures.

In the field of employment, some trade unions have developed guidelines for employers on protecting transgender people at work, such as the Dutch ABVAKABO and the UK trade union UNISON. In the Italian city of Torino a programme has been set up to reintegrate transgender people in employment after their gender reassignment surgery. (19) It consists of a distinct investigation of the needs and skills of the transgender person and gives options for temporary jobs in a number of companies, with the possibility of further permanent employment.

A few countries have developed high quality medical centres providing supportive care without resort to excessive psychiatric assessment procedures and giving health insurance coverage that includes all available forms of gender reassignment surgery and hormone treatment.

In the UK, Germany and the Netherlands there are support groups for children, teenagers and their parents who have questions around gender identity. Their work is crucial. However, there are not enough of these services available and the public funding for those that do exist is scarce, most are under constant threat of closure.

A few local school and university boards across Europe have acknowledged the need to address the high instances of bullying and exclusion experienced by transgender youth. For example, the UK Government Department for Children, Schools and Families is working with the major transgender support groups in the UK to produce guidance for schools on transphobic bullying. Moreover, the Centre for Excellence in Leadership has worked with a transgender rights group to publish a self-study course on transgender issues for senior staff and managers in colleges and other higher educational institutions. (20) Regarding the issue of university degrees and papers with the new name and sex of a transgender person, the University of Torino issues student identity cards with the chosen name before the legal name change has occurred in order to facilitate matters for transgender students.

In 2008 and 2009 European-wide research projects started on human rights of transgender persons. Some Council of Europe member states have started nation-wide research on the situation of transgender people. The European Commission is planning to publish in 2009 a report on transgender discrimination in EC law, which is being drafted by the EU Network of Legal Experts on Non-discrimination". And the year 2010 will hopefully lead to solid recommendations by the Council of Europe Committee of Ministers that should include, for the first time, gender identity-specific human rights concerns.

What is now needed in particular is promotion of a human rights approach to the challenges transgender people face. To help with this, educational campaigns promoting respect and mutual understanding are needed. The information deficit on the specific problems of trans-gender persons and the bullying and ridiculing they receive need to be addressed. The Commissioner's Office has launched a comparative study on the situation of LGBT persons in Council of Europe member states, and gender identity discrimination will have a prominent role in this research. The results are expected in autumn 2010.

It is important that gender identity discrimination be addressed by NHRSs and Equality Bodies. A good example of this is the 2006 New Zealand Human Rights Commission's report on discrimination experienced by transgender people. (21) In 2008, the Belgian Institute for Equality between Women and Men also launched a study on the situation of transgender persons in Belgium. The results are expected in 2009.

Support for civil society organisations promoting human rights of transgender persons, on the national and European level, is crucial for their ability to conduct lobby and advocacy activities. Only a handful of governments, such as the Netherlands, Norway and Scotland, have so far provided funding to transgender NGOs. The city councils of both Vienna and Berlin financially supported the first two European Transgender Councils in 2005 and 2008, which is currently the only specific forum for transgender people on a European level.

Finally, discussions are also needed to link the human rights of transgender persons to a variety of other debates and topics: violence against women, domestic violence, multiple discrimination, economic, cultural and social rights. A good example of this is the UK Public Sector Gender Equality Duty which requires all public authorities in the UK to eliminate unlawful discrimination and harassment on the grounds of sex and to promote equality of opportunity between women and men "including transsexuals of both genders". (22)

V. RECOMMENDATIONS TO COUNCIL OF EUROPE MEMBER STATES

Member states of the Council of Europe should:
1. Implement international human rights standards without discrimination, and prohibit explicitly discrimination on the ground of gender identity in national non-discrimination legislation. The Yogyakarta Principles on the Application of International Human Rights Law in relation to Sexual Orientation and Gender Identity should be used to provide guidance for national implementation in this field;

2. Enact hate crime legislation which affords specific protection for transgender persons against transphobic crimes and incidents;

3. Develop expeditious and transparent procedures for changing the name and sex of a transgender person on birth certificates, identity cards, passports, educational certificates and other similar documents;

4. Abolish sterilisation and other compulsory medical treatment as a necessary legal requirement to recognise a person's gender identity in laws regulating the process for name and sex change;

5. Make gender reassignment procedures, such as hormone treatment, surgery and psychological support, accessible for transgender persons, and ensure that they are reimbursed by public health insurance schemes;

6. Remove any restrictions on the right of transgender persons to remain in an existing marriage following a recognised change of gender;

7. Prepare and implement policies to combat discrimination and exclusion faced by transgender persons on the labour market, in education and health care;

8. Involve and consult transgender persons and their organisations when developing and implementing policy and legal measures which concern them;

9. Address the human rights of transgender persons and discrimination based on gender identity through human rights education and training programmes, as well as awareness-raising campaigns;

10. Provide training to health service professionals, including psychologists, psychiatrists and general practitioners, with regard to the needs and rights of

transgender persons and the requirement to respect their dignity;

11. Include the human rights concerns of transgender persons in the scope of activities of equality bodies and national human rights structures;

12. Develop research projects to collect and analyse data on the human rights situation of transgender persons including the discrimination and intolerance they encounter with due regard to the right to privacy of the persons concerned.

© *Council of Europe.*

1. Based on this article, how can governments best improve human rights for transgender people?

EXCERPT FROM "ADDRESSING SEXUAL ORIENTATION AND GENDER IDENTITY DISCRIMINATION IN FEDERAL CIVILIAN EMPLOYMENT: A GUIDE TO EMPLOYMENT RIGHTS, PROTECTIONS, AND RESPONSIBILITIES," BY THE OFFICE OF PERSONNEL MANAGEMENT, THE EQUAL EMPLOYMENT OPPORTUNITY COMMISSION, THE OFFICE OF SPECIAL COUNSEL, AND THE MERIT SYSTEMS PROTECTION BOARD, REV. JUNE 2015

INTRODUCTION

It is the policy of the Federal Government to provide equal employment opportunity to all individuals. Executive Order 11478, as amended, expressly prohibits discrimination based on sexual orientation and gender identity within executive branch civilian employment. It also prohibits discrimination based on race, color, religion, sex, national origin, disability, parental status, and age. The Executive Order states that this non-discrimination policy "must be an integral part of every aspect of personnel policy and practice in the employment, development, advancement, and treatment of civilian employees of the Federal Government, to the extent permitted by law."

There are a number of administrative and legal protections available to federal workers who believe they have been discriminated against because of their sexual orientation or gender identity, including:

- Title VII of the Civil Rights Act of 1964;
- Civil Service Reform Act of 1978; and/or
- Other Procedures.

Title VII's prohibition on sex discrimination protects persons who have been discriminated against based on sexual orientation and gender identity. Further, civil service laws prohibit certain employment decisions or personnel actions when the decisions or actions are based on conduct that does not adversely affect job performance, including sexual orientation and gender identity. In addition, individual agencies and unions may establish procedures to resolve disputes, including complaints of discrimination based on sexual orientation and gender identity.

This resource guide provides basic and general information about these various procedures and the circumstances under which federal applicants and employees may be able to take a particular course of action. Under some circumstances, more than one procedure may be available, and the choice of one procedure may preclude the use of others.

Most of the available avenues require employees to raise the allegations within a specific time frame from the date that the alleged discrimination occurred. The remedies available may also differ depending on the course of action that is chosen.

Federal employees should review the rules and processes specific to their agencies, and those issued by agencies that decide complaints and appeals, before deciding whether and how to proceed. Individuals also should consider consulting with an attorney experienced in federal employment issues or, where applicable, a knowledgeable union officer.

I. AGENCY RESPONSIBILITIES

As the nation's largest employer, the Federal Government should set an example for other employers that employment discrimination based on sexual orientation or gender identity is not acceptable. All federal workers—including lesbian, gay, bisexual, and transgender (LGBT) individuals—should be able to perform their jobs free from any unlawful discrimination.

Agencies, including federal officials and managers, should commit to promoting a work environment that is free from sexual orientation and gender identity discrimination, in accordance with existing federal law. Agencies should notify employees about avenues of redress and

KEY DEFINITIONS

Sexual orientation means one's emotional or physical attraction to the same and/or opposite sex.

Gender identity means one's inner sense of one's own gender, which may or may not match the sex assigned at birth. Different people choose to express their gender identity differently. For some, gender may be expressed through, for example, dress, grooming, mannerisms, speech patterns, and social interactions. Gender expression usually ranges between masculine and feminine, and some transgender people express their gender consistent with how they identify internally, rather than in accordance with the sex they were assigned at birth.

encourage them to report instances of discrimination to their supervisors and to the agency's Equal Employment Opportunity (EEO) office. When made aware of problems, managers should consult with their human resources office or agency legal counsel to ensure that appropriate steps are taken. All reports of sexual orientation or gender identity discrimination should be taken seriously and addressed promptly and properly. In some circumstances, this may involve taking corrective steps or disciplining those who discriminate, as applicable.

II. EMPLOYMENT RIGHTS AND PROTECTIONS

A.TITLE VII OF THE CIVIL RIGHTS ACT OF 1964 (EEOC AND AGENCIES)

Title VII of the Civil Rights Act of 1964 states, "All personnel actions affecting employees or applicants for employment . . . [in the Federal Government] . . . shall be made free from any discrimination based on race, color, religion, sex, or national origin." 42 U.S.C. §2000e-16(a). The Equal Employment Opportunity Commission (EEOC) is the agency charged with interpreting and enforcing Title VII in the Federal Government. The EEOC has recognized that Title VII's prohibition on sex discrimination provides protections for persons who have been discriminated against based on sexual orientation and gender identity.

EEOC AND AGENCIES—FILING A CLAIM UNDER THE
FEDERAL EEO PROCESS (29 C.F.R. PART 1614)

Individuals who believe they have been discriminated against based on sexual orientation or gender identity may file a complaint through their agency's federal sector EEO complaint process. The EEOC has instructed agencies to accept claims alleging sexual orientation or gender identity discrimination as claims of sex discrimination and to investigate those claims to determine if discrimination on the basis of sex occurred (including discrimination based on sex stereotypes).

B. CIVIL SERVICE REFORM ACT OF 1978 (OSC AND MSPB)

The Civil Service Reform Act of 1978 describes prohibited personnel practices. Two provisions prohibit discrimination based on sexual orientation and gender identity. First, 5 U.S.C. § 2302(b)(1) parallels Title VII's prohibitions against workplace discrimination based on sex. As described above, the EEOC has held that sex discrimination can include discrimination based on sexual orientation and gender identity. Second, 5 U.S.C. § 2302(b)(10) prohibits agencies from discriminating against employees based on conduct that does not adversely affect job performance. This prohibition has long been recognized as barring discrimination based on sexual orientation and gender identity.

When individuals believe that they have been subjected to a prohibited personnel practice based on sexual orientation or gender identity, they may seek assistance under certain circumstances from the U.S. Office of Special Counsel (OSC) and/or the Merit Systems Protection Board (MSPB).

OSC—FILING PROHIBITED PERSONNEL PRACTICE COMPLAINTS

OSC is an independent investigative and prosecutorial agency that investigates complaints alleging prohibited personnel practices, including those involving discrimination based on sexual orientation and gender identity. OSC often defers to the agencies' federal sector EEO complaint processes and the EEOC when an individual brings a claim under section 2302(b)(1).

MSPB—FILING CERTAIN PERSONNEL ACTION APPEALS

The MSPB is an independent, adjudicative agency that hears, among other things: (1) appeals of certain agency personnel actions brought by employees, former employees, or applicants, including removals, suspensions for more than 14 days, and reductions in grade and pay of certain federal employees who possess tenure; and (2) complaints brought by OSC involving prohibited personnel practices (see above).

C. OTHER PROCEDURES (UNIONS AND AGENCIES)

NEGOTIATED GRIEVANCE PROCEDURES

If employees think they have been the victims of sexual orientation or gender identity discrimination, they may also wish to contact their union.

Employees who are in a certified bargaining unit— that is, who are represented by a duly recognized labor organization and covered by a collective bargaining agreement—may file grievances in accordance with 5 U.S.C. § 7121.

AGENCY-SPECIFIC PROCEDURES

Another possible area of redress for those who believe they have been discriminated against based on their sexual orientation or gender identity is the availability of any agency-specific procedures.

Many agencies have their own systems to resolve disputes between an employee and the agency that may not be available elsewhere. In general, these systems try to achieve an informal resolution so that disputes do not have to be decided by higher levels of management. Specific procedures and time limitations vary by agency.

An employee considering such procedures must become familiar with the rules governing the particular agency's system. Employees who believe that they have been discriminated against due to their sexual orientation or gender identity should ask their human resource office for a copy of their agency procedures to determine the procedures to follow and subjects they cover.

III. OTHER PROCEDURAL ISSUES

ELECTION OF REMEDIES

Federal applicants and employees may seek protection from discrimination based on sexual orientation or gender identity under both Title VII and the Civil Service Reform Act. In other words, they may file EEO complaints and complaints of prohibited personnel practices.

As discussed above, while an individual may file both types of complaints, the complaint alleging a prohibited personnel practice must proceed under one and only one of the following processes:

- OSC;
- MSPB;
- Negotiated grievance procedures; or
- Agency-specific procedures.

The processes for each of these routes are described above in this resource guide. Individuals choosing to proceed should be careful to select the best process for them.

CONCLUSION

We hope that this resource guide will provide some important information to those who believe they have been the victims of discrimination based on sexual orientation or gender identity.

This resource guide should be widely distributed to federal workers and should be made available for review in central locations. Dissemination of information on procedural remedies is of great importance to individuals who may feel victimized by discrimination. But of primary importance is creating an atmosphere of fairness to applicants and employees. They should be secure in the knowledge that the federal agency for which they work will not treat them differently or less favorably on account of sexual orientation, gender identity, or any other consideration unrelated to merit.

Through the equitable treatment of all applicants and employees, the Federal Government can set an example for the nation that we serve.

1. What steps might federal employees take when they are discriminated against due to their gender identity?

EXCERPT FROM "GUIDANCE REGARDING THE EMPLOYMENT OF TRANSGENDER INDIVIDUALS IN THE FEDERAL WORKPLACE," BY THE US OFFICE OF PERSONNEL MANAGEMENT

POLICY AND PURPOSES

It is the policy of the Federal Government to treat all of its employees with dignity and respect and to provide a workplace that is free from discrimination whether that discrimination is based on race, color, religion, sex (including gender identity or pregnancy), national origin, disability, political affiliation, marital status, membership in an employee organization, age, sexual orientation, or other non-merit factors. Agencies should review their anti-discrimination policies to ensure that they afford a non-discriminatory working environment to employees irrespective of their gender identity or perceived gender non-conformity.

The purpose of this memorandum is to provide guidance to address some of the common questions that agencies have raised with OPM regarding the employment of transgender individuals in the federal workplace.

Because the guidance is of necessity general in nature, managers, supervisors, and transitioning employees should feel free to consult with their human resources offices and with the Office of Personnel Management to seek advice in individual circumstances.

CORE CONCEPTS

Gender identity is the individual's internal sense of being male or female. The way an individual expresses his or her gender identity is frequently called "gender expression," and may or may not conform to social stereotypes associated with a particular gender.

Transgender: Transgender individuals are people with a gender identity that is different from the sex assigned to them at birth. Someone who was assigned the male sex at birth but who identifies as female is a *transgender woman*. Likewise, a person assigned the female sex at birth but who identifies as male is a *transgender man*. Some individuals who would fit this definition of transgender do not identify themselves as such, and identify simply as men and women, consistent with their gender identity. The guidance discussed in this memorandum applies whether or not a particular individual self-identifies as transgender.

Transition: Some individuals will find it necessary to transition from living and working as one gender to another. These individuals often seek some form of medical treatment such as counseling, hormone therapy, electrolysis, and reassignment surgery. These treatments may be deemed medically necessary for many individuals, based on determinations of their medical providers.

Some individuals, however, will not pursue some (or any) forms of medical treatment because of their age, medical condition, lack of funds, or other personal circumstances, or because they may not feel the treatment is necessary for their well-being. Managers and supervisors should be aware that not all transgender individuals will follow the same pattern, but they all are entitled to the same consideration as they undertake the transition steps deemed appropriate for them, and should all be treated with dignity and respect.

TRANSITION WHILE EMPLOYED

There are several issues that commonly generate questions from managers and employees who are working with a transitioning employee. In order to assist you in ensuring that transitioning employees are treated with dignity and respect, we offer the following guidance on those issues.

Confidentiality and Privacy: An employee's transition should be treated with as much sensitivity and confidentiality as any other employee's significant life experiences, such as hospitalization or family difficulties. Employees in transition often want as little publicity about their transition as possible. They may be concerned about safety and employment issues if other people or employers become aware that he or she has transitioned. Moreover, medical information received about individual employees is protected under the Privacy Act (5 U.S.C. 552a).

Employing agencies, managers, and supervisors should be sensitive to these special concerns and advise employees not to spread information concerning the employee who is in transition: gossip and rumor-spreading in the workplace about gender identity are inappropriate. Other employees may be given only general information about the employee's transition; personal information about the employee should be considered confidential and should not be released without the employee's prior agreement. Questions regarding the employee should be referred to the employee himself or herself. It should be noted, however, that questions regarding a coworker's medical process, body, and sexuality are inappropriate. If it would be helpful and appropriate, employing agencies may have a trainer or presenter meet with employees to answer general questions regarding gender identity. Issues that may arise should be discussed as soon as possible confidentially between the employee and his or her managers and supervisors.

Dress and Appearance: Agencies are encouraged to evaluate, and consider eliminating, gender-specific dress and appearance rules. Once an employee has informed management that he or she is transitioning, agency dress codes should be applied to employees transitioning to a different gender in the same way that they are applied to other employees of that gender. Dress codes should not be used to prevent a transgender employee from living full-time in the role consistent with his or her gender identity.

Names and Pronouns: Managers, supervisors, and coworkers should use the name and pronouns appropriate to the gender the employee is now presenting at work. Further, managers, supervisors, and coworkers should take care to use the correct name and pronouns in employee records and in communications with others regarding the employee. Continued intentional misuse of the employee's new name and pronouns, and reference to the employee's former gender by managers, supervisors, or coworkers is contrary to the goal of treating transitioning employees with dignity and respect, and creates an unwelcoming work environment. Such misuse may also breach the employee's privacy.

Sanitary and Related Facilities: The Department of Labor's Occupational Safety and Health Administration (DOL/OSHA) guidelines require agencies to make access to adequate sanitary facilities as free as possible for all employees in order to avoid serious health consequences. For a transitioning employee, this means that, once he or she has begun working in the gender that reflects his or her gender identity, agencies should allow access to restrooms and (if provided to other employees) locker room facilities consistent with his or her gender identity. Transitioning employees should not be required to have undergone or to provide proof of any particular medical procedure (including gender reassignment surgery) in order to have access to facilities designated for use by a particular gender. Under no circumstances may an agency require an employee to use facilities that are unsanitary, potentially unsafe for the employee, located at an unreasonable distance from the employee's work station, or that are inconsistent with the employee's gender identity. Agencies are encouraged to provide unisex, single-user restrooms when feasible to maximize comfort and access for everyone, including individuals with disabilities and those with young children, however transgender employees should not be limited to using these facilities. Because every workplace is configured differently, agencies with questions regarding employee access to any facilities within an agency may contact OPM for further guidance.

Workplace Assignments and Duties: In some workplaces, specific assignments or duties are differentiated by gender. For a transitioning employee, once he or she has begun working full-time in the gender that reflects his or her gender identity, agencies should treat the employee as that gender for purposes of all job assignments and duties. Transitioning employees should not be required to have undergone or to provide proof of any particular medical procedure (including gender reassignment surgery) in order to be eligible for gender-specific assignments or duties. Under no circumstances may an agency require an employee to accept a gender-specific assignment or duty contrary to the gender the employee otherwise works as, or limit gender-specific assignments or duties for an employee once the employee's Official Personnel Folder (OPF) has been reconstructed to reflect the new gender.

Recordkeeping: Consistent with the Privacy Act, the records in the employee's Official Personnel Folder (OPF) and other employee records (pay accounts, training records, benefits documents, and so on) should be changed to show the employee's new name and gender, once the employee has begun working full-time in the gender role consistent with the employee's gender identity and has submitted a request to update his or her OPF. See 5 U.S.C. 552a(d).

Sick and Medical Leave: Employees receiving treatment as part of their transition may use sick leave under applicable regulations. Employees who are qualified under the Family Medical Leave Act may also be entitled to take medical leave for transition-related needs of their families.

Hiring Process: During the hiring process, hiring managers and supervisors should be sensitive to the possibility that applicants have transitioned. The name and gender on the application may correspond with the person's current usage; however, background or suitability checks may disclose a previous name that indicates a gender different from the one the applicant is currently presenting. In such cases, hiring managers should respectfully ask whether the applicant was previously known by a different name, and confirm with the applicant the name and gender that should be used throughout the hiring process.

Insurance Benefits: Employees in transition who already have Federal insurance benefits must be allowed to continue their participation, and new employees must be allowed to elect participation, based on their updated names and genders. If the employees in transition are validly married at the time of the transition, the transition does not affect the validity of that marriage, and spousal coverage should be extended or continued even though the employee in transition has a new name and gender. Further information about insurance coverage issues can be found on the web at OPM's Insure website, or by contacting the relevant OPM insurance program office.

Specific Questions: For further guidance on these issues, contact the Diversity Program Manager, Office of Diversity and Inclusion, Office of Personnel Management, 1900 E Street, NW, Washington, DC 20415, at (202) 606-0020.

1. How should employers treat transgender employees who are in the process of transitioning?

"THE POPE'S TAKE ON TRANSGENDER ISSUES? ACCEPT THE BODY GOD GAVE YOU," FROM THE CATHOLIC NEWS AGENCY, JUNE 18, 2014

Pope Francis' new encyclical on the environment calls for men and women to acknowledge their bodies as a gift from God which should not be manipulated.

"The acceptance of our bodies as God's gift is vital for welcoming and accepting the entire world as a gift from the Father and our common home," the Pope wrote, "whereas thinking that we enjoy absolute power over our own bodies turns, often subtly, into thinking that we enjoy absolute power over creation."

The Pope's encyclical "Laudato Si," meaning "Praise be to You," was published Thursday, June 18. Its name is taken from St. Francis of Assisi's medieval Italian prayer "Canticle of the Sun," which praises God through elements of creation like Brother Sun, Sister Moon, and "our sister Mother Earth."

In early 2014, the Vatican announced the Pope's plans to write on the theme of "human ecology"—a phrase that was previously used by Pope emeritus Benedict XVI.

While the 184-page encyclical wades into controversial topics such as climate change, it also aggressively argues that it is not possible to effectively care for the environment without first working to defend human life and dignity.

The Pope wrote that human ecology implies the profound reality of "the relationship between human life and the moral law, which is inscribed in our nature and is necessary for the creation of a more dignified environment."

Pope Francis quoted from his predecessor, Benedict XVI, saying that there is an "ecology of man" because "man too has a nature that he must respect and that he cannot manipulate at will."

Benedict's words came from his Sept. 22, 2011 address to the German parliament on the foundations of law. He had discussed the importance of the ecological movement for its realization that "the earth has a dignity of its own and that we must follow its directives." Man, he added, "does not create himself. He is intellect and will, but he is also nature, and his will is rightly ordered if he respects his nature, listens to it and accepts himself for who he is, as one who did not create himself."

After quoting Benedict, Pope Francis said that "our body itself establishes us in a direct relationship with the environment and with other living beings," and that the acceptance of one's body helps one to accept and honor the entire world as a gift.

"Learning to accept our body, to care for it and to respect its fullest meaning, is an essential element of any genuine human ecology."

He then turned to the importance of sexual complementarity, adding that "valuing one's own body in its femininity or masculinity is necessary if I am going to be able to recognize myself in an encounter with someone who is different. In this way we can joyfully accept the specific gifts of another man or woman, the work of God the Creator, and find mutual enrichment."

Pope Francis referred to his own General Audience address of April 15, saying that "It is not a healthy attitude which would seek 'to cancel out sexual difference because it no longer knows how to confront it.'"

In that address, on the complementarity of man and woman, he had touched on the importance of the two sexes and their reciprocal needs.

He lamented that contemporary culture has introduced doubt and skepticism over sexual complementarity: "For example, I ask myself, if the so-called gender theory is not, at the same time, an expression of frustration and resignation, which seeks to cancel out sexual difference because it no longer knows how to confront it ... the removal of difference in fact creates a problem, not a solution."

Pope Francis' jab at gender theory—which gives a basis for transgender identification—in his encyclical came in the context of a discussion on the "ecology of daily life," during which he also discussed integral improvement in the quality of human life; creativity in responding to one's environment; the brutality arising from poverty; urban planning; lack of housing; public transportation; and rural life.

The larger context of the Pope's words on the ecology of daily life came in his chapter on integral ecology, during which he also mentioned environmental, economic, and social ecology; cultural ecology; the common good; and inter-generational justice.

1. What do you think about the belief, as expressed by Pope Francis and others in the Catholic Church, that sexual difference exists to fulfill the opposite sex's "reciprocal needs"? What would be the negatives of defining groups of people and their needs based solely on their biology?

"WHY CONSERVATIVE CHRISTIANS FEAR THE AFFIRMATION OF TRANSGENDER IDENTITY," BY DIANNA E. ANDERSON, FROM *RH REALITY CHECK*, SEPTEMBER 9, 2014

At its annual meeting this past June, the Southern Baptist Convention (SBC)—one of the largest Christian denominations in the world—passed a landmark resolution on the issue of transgender rights, making its stance on trans* people an official part of the doctrine.

The resolution says, in part, that SBC's leaders "condemn acts of abuse or bullying committed against [transgender individuals]." But they also resolve that no efforts should be made to "alter one's bodily identity (e.g. cross-sex hormone therapy, gender reassignment surgery) to bring it in line with one's perceived gender identity," and that they "continue to oppose steadfastly all efforts by any court or state legislature to validate transgender identity as morally praiseworthy."

In other words, even as the SBC ostensibly condemns physical aggression against trans* individuals, it has resolved to support state and institutional violence against the same people.

Visibility for trans* individuals has notably increased over the last decade, with the last two years in particular ushering in a skyrocketing amount of press and media aimed at trans* celebrities. Several prominent artists—musician Laura Jane Grace and director Lana Wachowski, for instance—came out as transgender women; Emmy-nominated actress and trans woman Laverne Cox appeared on the cover of *Time* magazine this June. And as the nation begins to look at LGBT rights with a wider lens, many prominent members of America's conservative Christian churches have begun to shift their focus as well.

Several popular leaders of these denominations have brought transgender issues to the forefront of their rhetoric and teachings. Unfortunately, this shift in focus comes largely without corresponding education, resulting in skewed, transphobic sermons. Most famously, the president of SBC's Ethics and Religious Liberty Commission, Russell Moore, wrote in 2009 about the ethical quandary that "repentant" transgender individuals posed for a pastor. Moore came to the conclusion that pastors should encourage people to embrace a gender identity that matches their assigned sex at birth and that transgender identity is, first and foremost, a sin.

In more recent years, Denny Burk, professor of biblical studies at Boyce College in Louisville, Kentucky, has apparently resolved to set himself up as SBC's resident "expert" on transgender identity. Unfortunately, Burk's writing mangles even the easiest explanations: He continuously uses "transgender" as a noun rather than an adjective, for example, and purposefully misgenders trans* individuals. The misgendering, in particular, seems to extend from a desire to "correct" others on their gender by reminding them of the one they were assigned at birth—a possible manifestation of many SBC leaders' proposed method of "loving" trans* people.

Overall, the religious right's recent push against transgender identity has been led by white, straight, cisgender men—and it has developed political implications outside the church. Shortly following the Supreme Court's *Hobby Lobby* decision in June, the heads of numerous religiously affiliated organizations wrote a letter to President Obama asking for similar exemptions to his recent executive order barring federal contractors from discriminating against the LGBT community in the workplace. In fact, this letter specifically objected to the idea of transgender inclusion.

One of the most notable of these signatories was D. Michael Lindsay, president of the evangelical Gordon College in Wenham, Massachusetts. Lindsay's move in signing the letter has led some alumni of the college to return their diplomas in protest, indicating that the anti-trans* sentiment is largely a generational gap.

But Gordon is not the first Christian college to embroil itself in controversy regarding transgender students. George Fox University, a Quaker school in the liberal bastion of Portland, Oregon, also found itself in hot water with activists this summer when it refused a transgender student the opportunity to live with his male friends.

The questions of religious exemptions and the liberty to practice religion as one sees fit are complex and complicated—far too much to go into here. One aspect of this quickly moving battle for both civil rights and understanding, however, is the theological ground for rejecting transgender identity.

Simply put: Conservative Christians are standing on shifting sands.

The Bible doesn't speak directly to transgender identity. So leaders on the religious right get around this by conflating non-binary gender with sexual sin—namely, "sexual immorality," a vague umbrella term covering everything from sex outside of marriage to homosexual acts. Gender, in the eyes of evangelicals, determines sexuality: If you are a man, it is your God-given role to marry and bed a woman. If you are a woman, you are to submit yourself to your husband. All other deviations from this norm are sin.

Without fixed gender, one's sexuality is therefore unstable. And fixed sexual and gendered roles are a necessity for the evangelical vision of family and church.

This series of assumptions is at the root of the evangelical fear of both marriage equality and transgender acceptance. The cultural hegemony that conservative Christian culture enjoyed for barely a generation is eroding, and with it the power evangelicals had to adapt the world to their whims. The very existence of gender outside a binary puts fear in the hearts of evangelicals because their narrow theology is dependent upon them: male and female, good and evil, heaven and hell. But since the Bible doesn't speak directly to the topic—the most we see is discussion of eunuchs—evangelicals must figure out a way to make transgender identity a sin of sexuality, forever muddying and confusing the issue.

In an August 2014 article for *9 Marks* journal, for instance, Southern Baptist Theological Seminary President R. Albert Mohler Jr. addresses the issue of transgender identity by addressing sexual sin, arguing that the physical body is vital "to our personhood," and as embodied creatures of God, a fixed gender is therefore necessary for human reproduction and, in turn, playing out the creation drama in which God placed us. Mohler admits that the Bible does not speak to transgender identity; therefore he must connect it to the evangelical concept of family—that reproduction is part of God's plan for everyone—in order to speak against it.

And in *Good*, an eBook recently released by celebrity pastor John Piper's Desiring God ministry, Burk continues his quest to undercut trans* identity, writing:

> We must tell the truth about what the Bible teaches about gender. Among other things, the Bible is clear that there is a normative connection between biological sex and gender identity. The "normative connection" I am speaking of is not defined by the sociological observation that a certain percentage of the population experiences their own gender in a that conflicts with their biological sex. The sociological norm knows nothing of the Fall and confuses what *is* with what *ought* to be. The norm that we must insist on is the norm that is not normed by any other norm: Scripture.

Amidst that word salad, what Burk is essentially saying is that while transgender identity may occur as a sociological and statistical reality, such "realities" don't take into account the influence of sin and the fall of man into evil; therefore, sociological facts don't represent the kingdom of God as what *should* be. In other words, Burk recognizes that transgender people exist as a matter of course, but he doesn't care because the scripture—which he does not cite—allegedly says they shouldn't.

This is the theological basis for denying the rights of real people who survive in the real world: that they don't match up with an eschatological conception of life without sin, and therefore should be rejected and discriminated against. Any person who is unrepentantly trans*—who does not flagellate themselves before the altar of the binary and biologically determined gender—is therefore acting in open defiance to God's good law about gender. And sinning so openly means discrimination is the only holy response.

Such a belief is so dependent upon a number of evaporating cultural assumptions—straight marriage that will always produce children, gender and sexuality as fixed states, the idea that men are leaders and women are followers—that it's fairly easy to see why representatives of various Christian organizations are panicked at the idea of affirming transgender identities. That affirmation, after all, would be a devastating blow for the house of cards upon which they've built their faith. Accepting the very existence of trans* people is an act that threatens their image of God—because God, in conservative Christians' eyes, only created (and called "good") male and female in a compulsory heterosexual binary.

And yet, this is precisely why trans* visibility and laws protecting trans* identities are so important.

One shouldn't have to engage in an in-depth theological debate simply to exist as the person they are. One shouldn't have to make a theological case simply to justify why they should be allowed to hold a job or attend the college of their choosing. But this is the reality for many trans* Christians today—even if it is a house of cards, evangelicals are still fighting with all their might to keep it standing.

1. In your opinion, can the question of gender identity be brought into accord with the Christian faith?

CHAPTER 3

WHAT THE COURTS SAY

The gender binary is ingrained very deeply in society, and not conforming to the concept that a person has to be either male or female and has to stay that way from the day they were born until the day they die can lead to problems— especially in regards to a transgender person's legal status. In many situations, society is not prepared to deal with transgender people, and the bureaucratic insistence to adhere to categories that do not apply to some individuals can make their lives difficult. Often a court has to decide to create a precedent of how these situations, which range from discrimination in the workplace and the treatment of transgender people in prison to the ramifications of gender identity on marriage, are to be handled. This chapter covers recent American court cases, legal precedents set in the United States' courts and abroad, and a recent legal victory for transgender rights in the state of California.

EXCERPT FROM "SEXUAL ORIENTATION, GENDER IDENTITY AND JUSTICE: A COMPARATIVE LAW CASEBOOK," FROM THE INTERNATIONAL COMMISSION OF JURISTS, 2011

TRANSGENDER MARRIAGE: INTRODUCTION

Transgender marriage occurs when a change of gender identity is judicially recognised in the context of marriage. Since marriage in the majority of jurisdictions is defined in terms of opposite-sex partners, courts ask whether an individual is a man or a woman for the purpose of the marriage statute. What does it mean to be male or female? (1) Is a person's sex a biological fact, a legal construction, or a bit of both? Is one's capacity to marry defined by the ability to engage in penile-vaginal sex? Or is the ability to procreate determinative? These are the questions that courts seek to answer.

There is a great lack of consistency. Some courts reject the notion that a person can be legally recognised in a new sex for the purpose of marriage, even if that person has been recognised in the new sex for other purposes. Other courts apply various tests of sexual functionality or physical appearance. Because of the medical risks involved in the surgical construction of male genitalia, physical appearance tests are significantly harder for transgender men to meet than transgender women.

Transgender marriage cases are dominated by the 1970 British decision on *Corbett v. Corbett*. (2) In some sense, all transgender marriage cases are either an extension of *Corbett* reasoning or a reaction to it. (3) *Corbett* concerned a petition to legally annul the marriage between Arthur Corbett and April Ashley. April Ashley was born male and had undergone hormonal treatment and sex reassignment surgery, including vaginoplasty. According to Justice Omrod, the issue before him was the "true sex" of April Ashley and, secondarily, whether she had the capacity to consummate the marriage. He held that sex was determined by a congruence of chromosomal, gonadal and genital factors, and was a biological fact, determined at birth, forever immutable. In his view, April Ashley was physically incapable of consummating the marriage because intercourse using "the completely artificial cavity constructed" by a doctor could not possibly be described as natural intercourse. The outcome of *Corbett* was codified by the enactment of the *Nullity of Marriage Act 1971* and the *Matrimonial Causes Act 1973*. With his ruling, a single judge of the High Court set the terms of the debate for transgender marriage jurisprudence

MT v. JT, decided in 1976 by the Superior Court of New Jersey (USA), marked a significant departure from *Corbett.* Following their separation, MT petitioned for support and maintenance from her husband. MT had been born male and, prior to the marriage, had undergone "surgery for the removal of male sex organs and construction of a vagina." JT argued in defence that MT was male and that the marriage was invalid. The court ruled that the marriage was valid, stating "we must disagree with the conclusion reached in *Corbett* that for purposes of marriage sex is somehow irrevocably cast at the moment of birth, and that for adjudging the capacity to enter marriage, sex in its biological sense should be the exclusive standard". In reaching this conclusion, the court explained that it had a different understanding of sex and gender. It defined gender as "one's self-image, the deep psychological or emotional sense of sexual identity and character". In short, when an individual's "anatomical or genital features" were adapted to conform with a person's "gender, psyche or psychological sex", then identity by sex must be governed by the congruence of these standards.

MT v. JT also emphasised MT's capacity to function sexually as a female. The court stated that sexual capacity "requires the coalescence of both the physical ability and the psychological and emotional orientation to engage in sexual intercourse as either a male or a female". Medical witnesses testified that MT could no longer be considered male because "she could not function as a male sexually for purposes of recreation or procreation". Sexual capacity was thus determinative. Because MT had a vagina, she had the capacity to function sexually as a female and she should be legally recognised as a female for purposes of marriage. One commentator has described the relationship between *Corbett* and *MT v. JT* as the journey from "(bio)logic to functionality". (4)

Since *MT v. JT,* US courts have arrived at various and contradictory conclusions on transgender marriage. Almost all the cases have quoted *Corbett* or cases that relied on *Corbett*. Even as US States have increasingly provided statutory instruments that make it possible to recognise a

change of sex on birth certificates and other identity documents, courts have refused to recognise such marriages as
valid, perhaps out of fear of condoning same-sex marriage.
(5) Thus in the case of *In re Simmons*, the marriage was
ruled invalid even though Robert Simmons had changed
his birth certificate to reflect his male sex. (6) Markedly
different reasoning is evidenced by US Board of Immigration Appeals in *In re Lovo-Lara.* The petitioner had changed
her birth certificate to the female sex and married a male
citizen of El Salvador. The Board found that her marriage
was valid in the State in which she was married because
she had met the legal requirements for changing her sex
on her birth certificate. Since the marriage was legal under
State law, the federal government was required to recognise it for immigration purposes.

MT v. JT has been influential in other jurisdictions. In *M v. M*, a New Zealand court heard an application to declare invalid a marriage between a male-to-
female (MtF) transgender person and a biological male,
following twelve years of marriage. (7) In this case Mrs.
M brought the application for invalidity, arguing that she
was and always had been male. She had undergone sex
reassignment surgery, involving the amputation of the
penis and both testes and the construction of a vagina.
The marriage had been consummated. The court noted
that Mrs. M was similar to Ashley Corbett. Both had been
born male, had had sex reassignment surgery, and their
chromosomal structures had not changed. The court did
not consider the length of the marriage or the fact that
the parties had " a continuing sexual relationship" to be
factors that distinguished the case from *Corbett*. Nevertheless, *Corbett* was not binding on a New Zealand court.

The court was sympathetic to the plight of an individual who would be trapped in "some kind of sexual twilight zone" if the change of sex were not recognised, but it also noted that sympathy alone could not resolve the question. In the end, the court declared the marriage valid, while acknowledging that there was "no simple medical test for the determining of which side of the sexual line a particular person falls". The court stated:

> [I]n the absence of any binding authority which requires me to accept biological structure as decisive, and indeed any medical evidence that it ought to be, I incline to the view that however elusive the definition of "woman" may be, the applicant came within it for the purposes of and at the time of the ceremony of marriage. (8)

In response to *M v. M*, the Attorney-General of New Zealand sought a declaratory judgment as to the validity of a marriage involving an individual who had undergone sex reassignment through surgery or hormone therapy or any other medical means. In *Attorney-General v. Family Court at Otahuhu*, the High Court of New Zealand moved beyond a functional assessment to assess the physical appearance of the individual, focusing on genitalia. The court observed that, before the discovery of chromosomes, the "obvious manifestations of breast and genitalia including a woman's vagina would have been considered conclusive". In rejecting the biological determinism of *Corbett*, the court noted that neither the ability to procreate nor the ability to have sexual intercourse were required in order to marry. The law of New Zealand no longer required that a marriage be consummated. It found the reasoning in *MT v. JT* and *M v. M* compelling.

The High Court stated that reconstructive surgery was necessary for recognition, but did not require the capacity to perform vaginal-penile intercourse. The Court noted that there were "many forms of sexual expression possible without penetrative sexual intercourse". To be capable of marriage, however, a couple must present themselves as having what appeared to be the genitals of a man and a woman. Anatomy was dispositive, but sexual capacity was not. This opinion had practical implications. The court noted that there was "no social advantage in the law not recognizing the validity of the marriage of a transsexual in the sex of reassignment". To hold otherwise would be to allow a MtF individual to contract a valid marriage with a woman, when to "all outward appearances, such would be same sex marriages".

In *In re Kevin*, the Family Court of Australia affirmed the validity of a marriage between Kevin, a female-to-male (FtM) transgender individual, and his wife, a biological female. (The court of appeals later accepted the reasoning of the trial court in its entirety.) Kevin's situation differed from the earlier cases discussed because, although he had undergone hormone therapy and some surgery, he had not had phalloplasty (surgical construction of the penis). The court recognised the complexity of the situation, stating that there was no "formulaic solution" for determining the sex of an individual for the purpose of marriage. Instead it outlined a variety of factors without assigning preeminence to any of them; a person's individual sex should be determined by "all relevant matters". In the end, what appeared to be dispositive was the fact that Kevin functioned socially as a man, was accepted as male by his colleagues, family and friends, and was the father to a child born during the marriage through ART. Like *Attorney General v. Family Court at Otahuhu*, the court also emphasised the policy benefits of recognising transgender individuals in the acquired gender. Failing to do so would lead to situations where a FtM individual would only be permitted to marry a man.

In re *Kevin*, the court pointed out what it considered to be the major fallacy underlying *Corbett*. The court there had adopted an "essentialist view of sexual identity", by assuming that "individuals have some basic essential quality that makes them male or female". The Australian court disagreed with this assumption.

> The task of the law is not to search for some mysterious entity, the person's "true sex", but to give an answer to a practical human problem … to determine the sex in which it is best for the individual to live.

In *W v. Registrar of Marriages*, a recent Hong Kong case, the issue was whether a trans woman who had had sex reassignment surgery could marry. She had successfully changed her permanent identity card but not her birth certificate. The court first considered whether the words "man" and "woman" in the *Marriage Ordinance* and *Matrimonial Causes Ordinance* could be construed to include a "post-operative transsexual individual in his or her acquired sex". It found this to be a question of statutory construction. The meaning of "man" and "woman" did not include individuals who had changed their sex.

According to the court, "the ability to engage in natural heterosexual intercourse" was an essential feature of marriage, regardless of whether the law had always permitted older people or infertile people to marry. The purpose of marriage was procreative. It noted, too, that allowing a post-operative transsexual to marry in his or her acquired gender "would be tantamount to sanctioning same sex marriage of a particular form". This would have implications for other forms of same-sex marriage. In short, it was "almost self-evident that all this must be a matter for the legislature and not for the court in the name of statutory interpretation."

The Hong Kong court further noted that courts in New Zealand, Australia and New Jersey, while departing from *Corbett*, had adopted very different tests. *MT v. JT* emphasised the capacity to function sexually. In New Zealand, the court held that genital appearance was dispositive. In Australia, Kevin had neither the capacity to engage in penile-vaginal intercourse nor male genitalia and yet was recognised as male, largely because of his self-perception and the perceptions of those around him. These varying circumstances, according to the court, also weighed in favor of a legislative solution. The court stated:

> It seems to me that at the highest, the applicant's case here is that 40 years after *Corbett*, because of the many changes that have taken place, there has now been opened a legislative gap, so far as our law of marriage is concerned, relating to the position of post-operative transsexuals. It is a gap that needs to be addressed one way or another. Yet it does not follow that it is for a court, in the name of statutory interpretation, to fill the gap. Given the inherent difficulties and potential ramifications involved, the gap is one

that is for the legislature to consider filling. The court has no mandate to do so.

As for the right to marry argument raised by the applicant, the court found that the definition of marriage was largely influenced by social consensus. It noted that non-consummation was still a ground for invalidating a marriage in Hong Kong and that, as a society, Hong Kong emphasised procreation. The applicant's argument, which prioritised mutual society, help and comfort over procreation, had potentially far-reaching implications and could open the door to same-sex marriage. "This shows that the problem one is dealing with cannot be answered by reference to logic or deduction alone, which is essentially what the present argument is all about; rather, it must be answered primarily by reference to societal understanding and acceptance". The court reframed the question: it was not about the restriction of a right "according to the wishes of the majority" but rather about whether the institution of marriage should be given a new contemporary meaning. Having held that the question was one of social consensus, the court found no violation of the right to marriage.

In 2002, the European Court of Human Rights, sitting as a Grand Chamber, effectively overruled *Corbett* and the *Matrimonial Causes Act* in the case of *Christine Goodwin v. United Kingdom*. In this instance, the applicant had been born male and had undergone hormone therapy, vocal chord surgery, and gender reassignment surgery. She alleged that, in refusing to change her social security card, national insurance card and birth certificate to reflect her female sex, the State had violated her right to respect for private life under Article 8 of the Convention. Furthermore, although she was in a relationship with a man, she could not marry her partner because the law treated her as a man, in violation of the right to marry under Article 12. The Court agreed.

The Court noted, first, that the applicant experienced stress and alienation that resulted from the "discordance" between her identity and her lack of legal recognition. It described this as a conflict between social reality and the law. "Serious interference with private life can arise where the state of domestic law conflicts with an important aspect of personal identity". (9) The Court rejected *Corbett's* assertion that sex was determined at birth on the basis of chromosomal, gonadal, and genital factors. It found that the chromosomal element should not "take on decisive significance for the purposes of legal attribution of gender identity". Departing from its previous case law, the Court concluded that Article 8 imposed a positive obligation on the State to legally recognise gender reassignment.

As for the right to marry claim, the Court held that inability to conceive a child did not vitiate the right to marry. (10) The applicant lived as a woman, was in a relationship with a man, and would only desire to marry a man. To deny her the possibility of doing so violated Article 12. (12)

The cases included here from New Zealand and Australia are unusual in that they played a role in influencing the reasoning of the European Court of Human Rights. The European Court explicitly relied on these decisions, as well as legislative developments in other countries, when it found an international trend towards legal recognition of changed gender identity. (12) The Court also found support from *In re Kevin* in rejecting chromosomes as a deciding factor. The thinking of the European Court was influenced in a third way, too: Strasbourg acknowledged the lived social reality of transgender individuals, which was also highlighted in the New Zealand and Australian cases. The key issue was not finding the "true sex" of an individual, but recognising the sex in which that person lived. The interplay between these decisions and the landmark case of *Christine Goodwin* emphasises the extent to which judicial conversations take place not only across borders but also between national and supranational courts.

1. How have recent court cases on transgender issues set new precedents or overturned the rulings of previous cases?

2. In following the progression of these global court cases, do you believe that legal progress has been made in the arena of transgender rights?

"FACT SHEET: RECENT EEOC LITIGATION REGARDING TITLE VII & LGBT-RELATED DISCRIMINATION," BY THE US EQUAL EMPLOYMENT OPPORTUNITY COMMISSION, LAST UPDATED AUGUST 27, 2015

OVERVIEW

The Commission adopted its current Strategic Enforcement Plan (SEP) in December of 2012. The SEP includes "coverage of lesbian, gay, bisexual and transgender individuals under Title VII's sex discrimination provisions, as they may apply" as a top Commission enforcement priority.

Consistent with this priority, the Commission's General Counsel formed an LGBT working group that provides advice and input to the Agency's litigators on developing related litigation vehicles. This work group also coordinates internal initiatives and policies, trains internal staff, and conducts outreach with external stakeholders.

In addition, Agency litigators have filed lawsuits and amicus curiae briefs in various courts addressing a multitude of LGBT-discrimination-related issues. These include:

PRIVATE SECTOR LITIGATION

EEOC v. Deluxe Financial Services Corp., (D. Minn. Civ. No. 0:15-cv-02646-ADM-SER, filed June 4, 2015). The EEOC sued Deluxe Financial Services Corporation, a check-printing and financial services corporation, alleging that after charging party, Britney Austin, began to present at work as a woman and informed her supervisors that she was transgender, Deluxe refused to let her use the women's restroom in violation of Title VII. The Commission further alleged that supervisors and coworkers subjected her to a hostile work environment, including hurtful epithets and intentionally using the wrong gender pronouns to refer to her.

EEOC v. Lakeland Eye Clinic, P.A. (M.D. Fla. Civ. No. 8:14-cv-2421-T35 AEP filed Sept. 25, 2014, settled April 9, 2015). The EEOC sued Lakeland Eye Clinic, an organization of health care professionals, alleging that it discriminated based on sex by firing an employee because she is transgender, because she was transitioning from male to female, and/or because she did not conform to the employer's gender-based expectations, preferences, or stereotypes in violation of Title VII. According to the EEOC's lawsuit, the defendant's employee had performed her duties satisfactorily throughout her employment. However, after she began to present as a woman and informed the clinic she was transgender, Lakeland fired her. In April 2015, Defendant agreed to settle the case by entering into a two year consent decree which includes injunctive relief and $150,000 in monetary damages.

EEOC v. R.G. & G.R. Harris Funeral Homes Inc. (E.D. Mich. Civ. No. 2:14-cv-13710-SFC-DRG filed Sept. 25, 2014). The EEOC sued Detroit-based R.G. & G.R. Harris Funeral Homes Inc., alleging that it discriminated based on sex by firing a funeral director/embalmer because she is transgender, because she was transitioning from male to female, and/or because she did not conform to the employer's gender-based expectations, preferences, or stereotypes in violation of Title VII. According to the EEOC's lawsuit, Amiee Stephens had been employed by Harris as a funeral Director/Embalmer since October 2007 and had always adequately performed the duties of that position. In 2013, she gave Harris a letter explaining she was undergoing a gender transition from male to female, and would soon start to present (e.g., dress) in appropriate business attire at work, consistent with her gender identity as a woman. Two weeks later, Harris's owner fired Stephens, telling her that what she was "proposing to do" was unacceptable. Defendant filed a motion to dismiss the complaint on November 19, 2014. The EEOC opposed the motion on December 10, 2014. On April 23, 2015, the court denied defendant's motion to dismiss. The court acknowledged that "even though transgendered/transsexual status is currently not a protected class under Title VII, Title VII nevertheless 'protects transsexuals from discrimination for failing to act in accordance and/or identify with their perceived sex or gender.'" *Id.* at 8. The court concluded that the EEOC had sufficiently pled a sex-stereotyping gender-discrimination claim under Title VII because the Commission alleged that Stephen's failure to conform to sex stereotypes was the driving force behind the funeral home's decision to fire Stephens. *Id.* at 14.

EEOC v. Boh Bros. Constr. Co. LLC (5th Cir. 11-30770). The Commission won a jury verdict in the amount of $451,000 in this Title VII enforcement action with evidence showing that Chuck Wolfe, the supervisor of an all-male construction crew, harassed Kerry Woods, one of his subordinates, and created a hostile work environment. The district court subsequently reduced the verdict to

$301,000 because of statutory limits and also provided injunctive relief to prevent future discrimination. A panel of the Fifth Circuit reversed the jury verdict, and the EEOC sought rehearing en banc. In September 2013, a 10-6 majority of the Court of Appeals upheld the jury verdict except for the punitive damages award.

The Appellate Court held that a plaintiff alleging same-sex harassment can show that the harassment occurred because of sex by showing that it was motivated by the harasser's subjective perception that the victim failed to conform to gender stereotypes. The Court agreed with the Commission that this rule follows from *Price Waterhouse v. Hopkins*, 490 U.S. 228 (1989), and *Oncale v. Sundowner Offshore Services, Inc.,* 523 U.S. 75 (1998). The Court ruled that the focus is on the "harasser's subjective perception of the victim" and even an employer's "wrong or ill-informed assumptions about its employee may form the basis of a discrimination claim" since "[w]e do not require a plaintiff to prop up his employer's subjective discriminatory animus by proving that it was rooted in some objective truth." The Court then ruled that the Commission had offered sufficient evidence to sustain the jury's verdict that Wolfe harassed Woods because of sex (here, because Wolfe viewed Woods as "not manly enough"), and that Wolfe's harassment of Woods was sufficiently severe or pervasive to create a hostile environment. *See* 732 F.3d 444 (5th Cir. 2013) (en banc).

PRIVATE SECTOR AMICUS BRIEFS

TRANSGENDER STATUS & GENDER-IDENTITY

Pacheco v. Freedom Buick GMC Truck, Inc. (W.D. Tex. Civ. No. 7:10-cv-00116) (amicus brief submitted as attachment with motion for leave to file Oct. 17, 2011; district court denied motion for leave to file Nov. 1, 2011). Plaintiff Alex Pacheco filed suit alleging that defendant Freedom Buick GMC Truck, Inc. discharged her because she is transgender and failed to conform to male gender stereotypes, and that this is discrimination because of sex in violation of Title VII. Freedom moved for summary judgment. The Commission sought to file an amicus curiae brief in which the Commission took the position that, as a matter of law, disparate treatment of an employee because she is transgender is discrimination because of sex. The amicus brief argued that this is so for at least two reasons: (1) under the reasoning of the Supreme Court's decision in *Price Waterhouse v. Hopkins*, 490 U.S. 228 (1989), discrimination against a transgender individual because he or she does not conform to gender norms or stereotypes is discrimination "because of . . . sex" under Title VII; and (2) following the reasoning in *Schroer v. Billington*, 577 F. Supp. 2d 293 (D.D.C. 2008), discrimination because an individual intends to change, is changing, or has changed his or her sex, is likewise prohibited by Title VII. The amicus brief also took the position that there were genuine issues of material fact that should preclude summary judgment on Pacheco's claim.

    The Commission filed a motion for leave to file this amicus brief in the district court, and attached a copy of the brief to this motion. Freedom opposed the EEOC's motion for leave to file. The district court entered an order denying Freedom's motion for summary judgment. Later, the district court entered a separate order denying the EEOC's motion for leave to file its amicus brief. However, the district court did not strike the EEOC's motion for leave to file (or the proposed amicus brief, which was attached to the EEOC's motion) from the public docket sheet for the case.

Chavez v. Credit Nation Auto Sales, LLC (N.D. Ga. No. 1:13-cv-0312) (amicus brief filed June 5, 2014). Plaintiff worked as a mechanic for Credit Nation, a company that sells and repairs cars. In 2009, she informed her employer that she intended to transition from male to female. Some months later, she was terminated after a supervisor photographed her sleeping in a car during working hours. She then filed suit under Title VII, alleging that she was fired because of her gender. In moving for summary judgment, defendant argued that the plaintiff did not exhaust her administrative remedies because she failed to file a timely charge. The Commission filed an amicus curiae brief in the district court, limited to this issue. The Commission argued that the charge-filing limitations period should be tolled because before finally accepting the plaintiff's charge, EEOC had twice refused on the ground that "transgendered persons cannot file claims for sex discrimination under Title VII."

In ruling on the summary judgment motion, the district court rejected defendant's exhaustion argument. Without mentioning EEOC's brief, the court noted that the "limitations period under Title VII may be equitably tolled if the EEOC misleads a complainant regarding the nature of his or her rights." In the court's view, that is what happened here. The court stated that "Title VII prohibits employers from discriminating against employees for failing to act and appear according to expectations defined by gender." (citing *Price Waterhouse v. Hopkins,* 490 U.S. 228, 235 (1989); *Glenn v. Brumby,* 683 F.3d 1312, 1316 (11th Cir. 2011)). The court reasoned that because the "'very acts that define transgender people as transgender are those that contradict stereotypes of gender-appropriate appearance and behavior, . . . [d]iscrimination against a transgender individual because of the gender nonconformity is sex discrimination, whether it's described as being on the basis of sex or gender.'" (citing *Brumby,* 683 F.3d at 1317) (adding that the "majority of federal courts" agree). Accordingly, the court concluded, "the EEOC misled [p]laintiff when it told [her] that she could not bring a claim for gender discrimination under Title VII," and, so, limitations on the claim "is required to be equitably tolled." The court went on to grant defendant's motion, however, finding no issue of fact as to whether the proffered reason for her termination - sleeping on the job - was pretextual. *See* 2014 WL 4585452 (N.D. Ga. Sept. 12, 2014).

Lewis v. Highpoint Reg'l Health Sys. (E.D.N.C. No. 5:13-cv-838-BO) (amicus brief filed Oct. 30, 2014). Plaintiff, a transgender female, alleges that defendant violated Title VII by failing to hire her in 2013 because of her sex/gender. Plaintiff alleges that during the interview process, she was interviewed by a group of peer nurses who ridiculed her regarding her sex. Defendant informed plaintiff that it was looking for someone with more experience. Although plaintiff had the qualifications for the position, she was not hired; rather, she alleges that an individual with less experience was hired for the position.

Defendant filed a motion to dismiss arguing that Title VII does not prohibit "sexual orientation" discrimination.

In an amicus brief, the EEOC argued the district court should deny defendant's motion to dismiss and hold that failing to hire an individual because she is transgender violates Title VII. The EEOC explained that sexual orientation is a different concept altogether than transgender status or gender identity. The EEOC further explained that courts have recognized that Title VII's prohibition on sex discrimination encompasses discrimination based on the failure to conform to gender expectations. Thus, discrimination against a transgender individual for non-conformance with gender norms is sex discrimination. Further, the EEOC argued, specific evidence of gender stereotyping is not necessary because consideration of gender stereotypes is inherently part of what drives transgender discrimination.

On October 30, the district court granted the EEOC's motion for leave to file its amicus brief. The court noted that "[i]t is clear that this Court's ruling will implicate the interpretation and effective enforcement of Title VII, and therefore the EEOC has an interest in this matter. Further, as plaintiff is *pro se*, and the EEOC is the expert agency on the matter of Title VII, the EEOC's amicus brief will be of aid to the Court in its decisional process."

On January 15, 2015, the district court denied defendant's motion to dismiss (as well as plaintiff's motion for summary judgment). The court noted that "[n]owhere in her complaint does plaintiff allege discrimination on the basis of sexual orientation." Further, the court concluded, "neither the Supreme Court nor the Fourth Circuit's Title VII jurisprudence has addressed transgender status, which, as amicus EEOC points out, is different than sexual orientation." The Court declined to resolve whether "plaintiff's complaint fits within a gender-stereotyping framework" since "the issue was not raised in defendant's motion to dismiss . . . ." *See* 2015 WL 221615 (E.D.N.C. Jan. 15, 2015).

Jamal v. Saks & Co. (S.D. Tex. No. 4:14-cv-02782) (amicus brief submitted with motion for leave to file Jan. 22, 2015). Plaintiff, a transgender individual, alleges that defendant violated Title VII by harassing and discharging her because of her sex/gender. Plaintiff alleges that managers and co-workers referred to her using male pronouns, despite her requests to use female pronouns. Further, plaintiff alleges that management told her to change her appearance to a more masculine one, not to wear makeup or feminine clothing, and to separate her home life from her work life. She filed an EEOC charge and was fired ten days later. Defendant filed a motion to dismiss arguing that Title VII does not protect "transsexuals." Defendant further argued that plaintiff failed to comply with the administrative prerequisites to suit because her EEOC charge described her as a male yet her complaint used the pronoun "her." Finally, defendant argued that plaintiff could not state a claim for retaliation because she had no reasonable belief that the conduct she complained of violated Title VII.

In its proposed amicus brief, the EEOC argues that the district court should deny defendant's motion to dismiss and hold that discrimination against an individual because she is transgender violates Title VII. As it did in in its amicus brief in *Lewis* (above), the EEOC explains that courts recognize that Title VII's prohibition on sex discrimination encompasses discrimination based on the failure to conform to gender expectations. Thus, discrimination against a transgender individual for non-conformance with gender norms is sex discrimination. Further, the EEOC contends, specific evidence of gender stereotyping is not necessary because consideration of gender stereotypes is inherently part of what drives transgender discrimination. Additionally, the EEOC argues, the district court should hold that plaintiff's EEOC charge satisfied the administrative prerequisite to a suit alleging transgender discrimination, as the discrimination alleged in the charge is the same discrimination as that alleged in the complaint. Finally, the EEOC urges the district court to hold that plaintiff's act of filing a charge with the EEOC and opposing conduct that a reasonable person would believe is unlawful is protected activity for purposes of a retaliation claim. The EEOC explains that Title VII's "participation clause" protects an individual from retaliation for filing a charge, without limitation (e.g., a showing that plaintiff's charge was filed "in good faith"). Plaintiff's "opposition clause" claim also should proceed because she could have a good faith, reasonable belief that transgender-based discrimination violates Title VII.

On January 26, 2015, Saks withdrew its motion to dismiss plaintiff's claim. On March 4, 2015, the parties filed a stipulation agreeing to dismiss the action with prejudice.

SEXUAL ORIENTATION

Muhammad v. Caterpillar Inc. (7th Cir. No. 12-173) (amicus brief filed October 9, 2014). Plaintiff-Appellant Warnether Muhammad filed this Title VII suit against his employer Caterpillar, Inc., alleging that his co-workers created a sex-

and race-based hostile work environment. He also alleged that his supervisor unlawfully retaliated by suspending him after he complained about the harassment. The alleged harassment included anti-gay comments and conduct. The district court granted the defendant's motion for summary judgment on all claims. A panel of the U.S. Court of Appeals for the Seventh Circuit affirmed, in part on the grounds that Title VII does not prohibit sexual-orientation harassment, or retaliation against individuals who oppose it in the workplace. Muhammad petitioned for panel rehearing.

In an amicus curiae brief supporting the petition, the Commission argued that part of the panel's ruling rests on the sweeping proposition that Title VII's prohibition on discrimination "because of sex" does not prohibit discrimination based on sexual orientation. Yet an increasing number of courts, as well as the EEOC (the primary Agency charged with enforcing the statute), have recognized that intentional discrimination based on an individual's sexual orientation can be proved to be grounded in sex-based norms, preferences, expectations, or stereotypes. For example, in *Terveer v. Billington*, 2014 WL 1280301 (D.D.C. Mar. 31, 2014), the U.S. District Court for the District of Columbia held that a plaintiff's allegation that discrimination occurred because of "plaintiff's status as a homosexual" - without more - plausibly suggested the discrimination was based on gender stereotypes, and thus stated a Title VII *sex*-discrimination claim. Accordingly, Title VII's anti-retaliation rule protects individuals who in good faith oppose sexual-orientation discrimination in the workplace. The EEOC argued that for these reasons, the panel should modify the categorical statements to the contrary in its opinion, overruling the Circuit's precedent if necessary.

On October 16, 2014, the panel denied the petition for rehearing. But in a significant step, the panel issued an amended opinion removing its original rulings regarding the scope of Title VII coverage. The opinion no longer repeats or relies upon statements from prior Seventh Circuit decisions that Title VII does not prohibit sexual-orientation discrimination or retaliation for related opposition conduct. The revised panel opinion affirms the district court's summary-judgment for Caterpillar on other grounds, on which the Commission took no position. *See* 767 F.3d 694 (7th Cir. 2014), 2014 WL 4418649 (7th Cir. Sept. 9, 2014, as Amended on Denial of Rehearing, Oct. 16, 2014).

PUBLIC CONCILIATION AGREEMENTS

Don's Valley Market (public conciliation agreement announced Sept. 2013). A Rapid City, S.D. supermarket agreed to pay $50,000, obtain professional anti-discrimination training annually for all its employees, and provide a letter of apology and neutral reference (among other relief) to a former employee who was fired for being transgender. This resolution was reached as part of the EEOC's administrative conciliation process, without resort to litigation.

1. What specific legal issues do transgender people face?

"IN A FIRST, CALIFORNIA AGREES TO PAY FOR TRANSGENDER INMATE'S SEX REASSIGNMENT," BY PAIGE ST. JOHN, FROM THE *LOS ANGELES TIMES*, AUGUST 10, 2015

California is first in the nation to agree to pay for a transgender inmate's sex reassignment operation, but the state's settlement of a recent court case sidesteps the question of whether such surgery is a constitutional right.

The state concedes that Shiloh Quine, who entered the California prison system in 1980 as Rodney, suffers severe gender dysphoria that can be treated only by physically conforming her body to her psychological gender.

The agreement to settle Quine's federal lawsuit seeking the surgery was announced late Friday, with a brief statement from the corrections department that "every medical doctor and mental health clinician who has reviewed this case, including two independent mental health experts, determined that this surgery is medically necessary for Quine."

Quine's victory was made possible by another inmate, Michelle Norsworthy, born as Jeffrey, who in April won a federal court order for surgery to reshape her genitals. Gov. Jerry Brown on Friday allowed a parole grant for Norsworthy instead, making that ruling moot days before an appellate panel was to hear California's legal challenge.

In both instances, California prison officials had denied the surgeries, arguing that sex reassignment was not medically necessary. The state's position was undermined in June when its own expert concluded that Quine required the operation.

"Sex reassignment surgery is medically necessary to prevent Ms. Quine from suffering significant illness or disability, and to alleviate severe pain caused by her gender dysphoria," wrote Richard Carroll, a clinical psychologist and director of the Sexual Disorders and Couple Therapy Program at Northwestern University in Chicago. Surgery, he said, would reduce her "depression, anxiety and risk of suicide attempts."

Waiting until she got out of prison was not an option. Quine is serving a life sentence without parole for murder.

"A settlement is not a precedent, but I suppose it gives a little ammunition to the next guy, to say you did this for him, why not me?" said Kent Scheidegger, legal director for the Criminal Justice Legal Foundation, a conservative organization based in Sacramento that weighs in on criminal justice litigation across the nation. Those requests are bound to eventually force another legal challenge, he said.

"The idea that the 8th Amendment requires something for prisoners not available to the law-abiding public is something a lot of people find offensive," Scheidegger said.

California has nearly 400 transgender inmates receiving hormonal treatment, according to prison medical data. Quine's lawyers said their research shows the cost of the operation she seeks ranges from $15,000 to $25,000.

Litigation over surgery marks a "gigantic" progression in the rights of transgender inmates, said Valerie Jenness, dean of the School of Social Ecology at UC Irvine and a prominent researcher in the field. Her work documented the high incidence of sexual assault of transgender inmates in California, at nearly 60%.

"You can see the evolution," Jenness said.

California's settlement and Norsworthy's parole allow the state to avoid for now the danger of a higher court ruling putting sex-change surgeries on par with other medical procedures, with implications beyond the state's prisons.

Even without such a decision, Quine's lawyers said they believe the precedent has been set.

"This is clearly where the law is going and where the entire health industry is going," said Ilona Turner, legal director at the Transgender Law Center in Oakland, which handled the cases of Norsworthy and Quine. "These exclusions in health management plans are illegal."

The U.S. Department of Health and Human Services in May 2014 lifted its own exclusion on transgender services under Medicare, the national health insurance provider for seniors, allowing the tax-supported program to cover "gender-confirming" procedures endorsed by a patient's physicians.

Quine, who turned 56 on Friday, has been incarcerated since her Los Angeles County conviction in 1980 on first-degree murder, kidnapping and robbery. During that time, her legal filings show, she has repeatedly attempted suicide. In April 2014, a prison psychologist assessing Quine wrote that he believed sex reassignment was "reasonable and necessary to alleviate severe pain." When prison officials again denied the surgery, Quine in June 2014 tried once more to kill herself.

"I'm in severe pain," she wrote in a prison appeal after a state board recommended moving Quine to a maximum security unit. "I feel tortured and now being placed in future substantial risk of harm."

She has lived openly as a woman since 2008 and in 2009 began hormone treatment prescribed by her prison physicians. However, the prison system has denied her attempts to legally change her name, and she has filed numerous legal challenges seeking to require "sensitivity training" for prison officers and for officers to address her with feminine pronouns.

She is housed at Mule Creek State Prison, one of nine male institutions to which California sends transgender women. Transgender inmates often are housed apart from the general population in so-called sensitive needs yards, among child molesters, gang dropouts and others whose lives might be at risk.

Under Friday's settlement agreement, Quine will be moved to a women's prison if she completes surgery.

Until now, California has had only one other transgender woman inmate at a women's prison. The state's decision to reclassify and put Sherri Masbruch, a convicted rapist, among women caused an uproar in 2009. To this day, the California corrections department keeps her location secret, said corrections spokeswoman Terry Thornton. Prison officials in court have said Masbruch has been moved repeatedly in response to threats and assaults.

"Arranging for an inmate's sex reassignment surgery, providing the necessary security during hospitalization and ensuring that appropriate placement is available for both postoperative recovery and placement have no precedent in California's prison system, or in any other U.S. correctional environment of which I am aware," state prisons director Kelly Harrington said in a May deposition.

The issue of whether transgender inmates have a constitutional right to sex reassignment surgery was taken up by a federal judge in San Francisco, Jon Tigar, an appointee of President Obama.

Tigar had been on the bench less than two years last fall when he assigned himself to Quine's complaint and appointed a team of lawyers at a San Francisco firm and at the Transgender Law Center to represent her.

He already had Norsworthy's litigation before him. He noted the nation had yet to see a federal appeals court ruling on whether denying an inmate's doctor-prescribed sex change constituted "deliberate indifference" to a serious medical need. If it did, it would violate the 8th Amendment's bar on "cruel and unusual punishment."

At the time, Tigar said that precedent might be set on the East Coast, in the long-running litigation of Massachusetts transgender inmate Michelle Kosilek.

It took Kosilek a decade to win the right to hormone treatment in 2002. In early 2014, with supporting briefs from national organizations such as the American Civil Liberties Union, a panel of 1st Circuit Court of Appeals justices ruled that Kosilek, who had repeatedly tried to kill and to castrate herself, had a constitutional right to sex reassignment surgery as a medical necessity.

But two months later, a special panel of the Boston-based appellate court recalled that ruling and in December, the full court denied surgery to Kosilek. The majority opinion raised questions of prison security. Massachusetts had contended that a gender-reassigned Kosilek would be unsafe to house anywhere: a target for assault in a male prison, a source of mental distress for female inmates who had been victims of domestic abuse.

The state offered instead to provide suicide therapy if needed.

1. In your opinion, should a state have to pay for the treatment and gender reassignment surgery of prisoners suffering from gender dysphoria? Why or why not?

CHAPTER 4

WHAT ADVOCACY GROUPS SAY

There are numerous advocacy organizations that have the defined goal of providing information about transgender issues and working against prejudices and discrimination. To that end, they offer resources for people who want to learn about transgender issues, whether they are transgender themselves or not. These resources range from basic information about what gender and gender identity are, which is an important starting point for people who are just getting acquainted with the topic, to specific guides on how best to act in certain situations that can be problematic for a transgender person. For example, most people don't even have to think twice about using a public men's or women's bathroom, but this can be a stressful—and even dangerous—decision for a transgender person. In addition to this information, the articles in this chapter give advice on how people can get active and bring about change by campaigning to make public institutions like schools safer for transgender individuals.

"UNDERSTANDING GENDER," FROM GENDER SPECTRUM

For many people, the terms "gender" and "sex" are used interchangeably, and thus incorrectly. This idea has become so common, particularly in western societies, that it is rarely questioned. We are born, assigned a sex, and sent out into the world. For many people, this is cause for little, if any dissonance. Yet biological sex and gender are different; gender is not inherently nor solely connected to one's physical anatomy.

Biological Gender (sex) includes physical attributes such as external genitalia, sex chromosomes, gonads, sex hormones, and internal reproductive structures. At birth, it is used to assign sex, that is, to identify individuals as male or female. *Gender* on the other hand is far more complicated. It is the complex interrelationship between an individual's sex (gender biology), one's internal sense of self as male, female, both or neither (gender identity) as well as one's outward presentations and behaviors (gender expression) related to that perception, including their gender role. Together, the intersection of these three dimensions produces one's authentic sense of gender, both in how people experience their own gender as well as how others perceive it.

THE GENDER SPECTRUM

Western culture has come to view gender as a binary concept, with two rigidly fixed options: male or female, both grounded in a person's physical anatomy. When a child is born, a quick glance between the legs determines the gender label that the child will carry for life. But even if gender is to be restricted to basic biology, a binary concept still fails to capture the rich variation that exists. Rather than just two distinct boxes, biological gender occurs across a continuum of possibilities. This spectrum of anatomical variations by itself should be enough to disregard the simplistic notions of a binary gender system.

But beyond anatomy, there are multiple domains defining gender. In turn, these domains can be independently characterized across a range of possibilities. Instead of the static, binary model produced through a solely physical understanding of gender, a far richer tapestry of biology, gender expression, and gender identity intersect in a multidimensional array of possibilities. Quite simply, the gender spectrum represents a more nuanced, and ultimately truly authentic model of human gender.

FALLING INTO LINE

Gender is all around us. Like water surrounding creatures in the sea, we are often unaware of its ever-present nature. Gender is actually taught to us from the moment we are born. Gender expectations and messages bombard us constantly. Upbringing, culture, peers, schools, community, media, and religion are some of the many influences that shape our understanding of this core aspect of self. How you learned and interacted with gender as a young child directly influences how you view the world today. Gendered interactions between parent and child begin as soon as the sex of the baby is known. In short, many aspects of gender are socially constructed, particularly with regard to gender expression.

Like other social constructs, gender is closely monitored and reinforced by society. Practically everything in society is assigned a gender—toys, colors, clothes and behaviors are just some of the more obvious examples. Through a combination of social conditioning and personal preference, by age three most children prefer activities and exhibit behaviors typically associated with their sex. Accepted social gender roles and expectations are so entrenched in our culture that most people cannot imagine any other way. As a result, individuals fitting neatly into these expectations rarely if ever question what gender really means. They have never had to, because the system has worked for them.

ABOUT GENDER-EXPANSIVENESS

"Gender-expansive" is an umbrella term used for individuals that broaden commonly held definitions of gender, including its expression, associated identities, and/or other perceived gender norms, in one or more aspects of their life. These individuals expand the definition of gender through their own identity and/or expression. Some individuals do not identify with being either male or female; others identify as a blend of both, while still others identify with a gender, but express their gender in ways that differ from stereotypical presentations. A gender-expansive person's preferences and self-expression may fall outside commonly understood gender norms within their own culture; or they may be aligned with them even as one's internal gender identity doesn't align with the sex assigned at birth.

This diversity of gender is a normal part of the human experience, across cultures and throughout history. Non-binary gender diversity exists all over the world, documented by countless historians and anthropologists. Examples of individuals living comfortably outside of typical male/female expectations and/or identities are found in every region of the globe. The calabai, and calalai of Indonesia, two-spirit Native Americans, and the hijra of India all represent more complex understandings of gender than allowed for by a simplistic binary model.

Further, what might be considered gender-expansive in one period of history may become gender normative in another. One need only examine trends related to men wearing earrings or women sporting tattoos to quickly see the malleability of social expectations about gender. Even the seemingly intractable "pink is for girls, blue is for boys" notions are relatively new. While there is some debate about the reasons why they reversed, what is well documented is that not until the mid-twentieth century were notions of pink for girls or blue for boys so firmly ensconced. You can make the case that "pink is the new blue!"

GENDER AND PRIVILEGE

When someone is "typically gendered," they benefit from gender privilege. For individuals whose biological sex, gender expression, and gender identity neatly align, often referred to as "cisgender," there is a level of congruence as they encounter the world around them. Like many forms of social privilege, this is frequently an unexamined aspect of their lives. Forms they fill out, the clothing stores in which they shop, or identification papers they carry bring few if any second thoughts. Yet for a transgender or otherwise gender-expansive person, each of these, and many more examples, is a constant reminder that they move about in a culture that really does not account for their own experience. Social privilege comes from an assumption that one's own perspective is universal; whether related to race, or language, or gender, privilege comes from being part of the "norm." Or, as Dorothy Soelle aptly described it: Privilege is being able to choose what you will not see.

To understand this more intuitively, think about the last time you were in a public setting and needed to use a restroom. For cisgender individuals, this rarely presents a problem or question (issues of cleanliness notwithstanding!). Yet for an individual who does not fit into narrowly defined expectations of gender presentation or identity, restroom use can present a whole host of challenges, sometimes even becoming a matter of life and death. The daily need to make judgments about what one does, or wears, or says based on other people's perceptions of their gender is a burden that many people never encounter. These everyday reminders of being different are also constant reinforcement of being "other."

GENDER TERMINOLOGY

Given the complexity of gender, it is not surprising that an increasing number of terms and phrases are developing to describe it. Below are some of the key terms you might encounter:

Biological/Anatomical Sex. The physical structure of one's reproductive organs that is used to assign sex at birth. Biological sex is determined by chromosomes (XX for females; XY for males); hormones (estrogen/progesterone for females, testosterone for males); and internal and external genitalia (vulva, clitoris, vagina for assigned females, penis and testicles for assigned males). Given the potential variation in all of these, biological sex must be seen as a spectrum or range of possibilities rather than a binary set of two options.

Gender Identity. One's innermost concept of self as male or female or both or neither—how individuals perceive themselves and what they call themselves. One's gender identity can be the same or different than the sex assigned at birth. Individuals are conscious of this between the ages 18 months and 3 years. Most people develop a gender identity that matches their biological sex. For some, however, their gender identity is different from their biological or assigned sex. Some of these individuals choose to socially, hormonally and/or surgically change their sex to more fully match their gender identity.

Gender Expression. Refers to the ways in which people externally communicate their gender identity to others through behavior, clothing, haircut, voice, and other forms of presentation. Gender expression also works the other way as people assign gender to others based on their appearance, mannerisms, and other gendered characteristics. Sometimes, transgender people seek to match their physical expression with their gender identity, rather than their birth-assigned sex. Gender expression should not be viewed as an indication of sexual orientation.

Gender Role. This is the set of roles, activities, expectations and behaviors assigned to females and males by society. Our culture recognizes two basic gender roles: Masculine (having the qualities attributed to males) and feminine (having the qualities attributed to females). People who step out of their socially assigned gender roles are sometimes referred to as transgender. Other cultures have three or more gender roles.

Transgender. Sometimes used as an umbrella to describe anyone whose identity or behavior falls outside of stereotypical gender norms. More narrowly defined, it refers to an individual whose gender identity does not match their assigned birth gender. Being transgender does not imply any specific sexual orientation (attraction to people of a specific gender.) Therefore, transgender people may additionally identify with a variety of other sexual identities as well.

Sexual Orientation. Term that refers to being romantically or sexually attracted to people of a specific gender. Our sexual orientation and our gender identity are separate, distinct parts of our overall identity. Although a child may not yet be aware of their sexual orientation, they usually have a strong sense of their gender identity.

Gender Normative/Cisgender. Refers to people whose sex assignment at birth corresponds to their gender identity and expression.

Gender Fluidity. Gender fluidity conveys a wider, more flexible range of gender expression, with interests and behaviors that may even change from day to day. Gender fluid children do not feel confined by restrictive boundaries of stereotypical expectations of girls or boys. In other words, a child may feel they are a girl some days and a boy on others, or possibly feel that neither term describes them accurately.

CONCLUSION

Perhaps the most fundamental aspect of a person's identity, gender deeply influences every part of one's life. In a society where this crucial aspect of self has been so narrowly defined and rigidly enforced, individuals who exists outside its norms face innumerable challenges. Even those who vary only slightly from the norm can become targets of disapproval. Yet this does not have to be the case forever. Through a thoughtful consideration of the uniqueness and validity of every person's experiences of self, we can develop greater acceptance for all. Not only will this create greater inclusion for individuals who challenge the norms of gender, it will actually create space for all individuals to more fully explore and celebrate who they are.

1. What role does gender play in our lives?

2. Do you think gender categories are necessary? Why or why not?

EXCERPTS FROM "OPENING THE DOOR TO THE INCLUSION OF TRANSGENDER PEOPLE: THE NINE KEYS TO MAKING LESBIAN, GAY, BISEXUAL AND TRANSGENDER ORGANIZATIONS FULLY TRANSGENDER-INCLUSIVE," BY LISA MOTTET AND JUSTIN TANIS, FROM THE NATIONAL GAY AND LESBIAN TASK FORCE POLICY INSTITUTE AND THE NATIONAL CENTER FOR TRANSGENDER EQUALITY, 2008

INTRODUCTION

Thank you for picking up this guide and for your desire to discover new ways to help your lesbian, gay, bisexual and transgender (LGBT) organization become a more inclusive place for transgender people. It is exciting to see the ways in which our movement continues to grow and challenge ourselves to be more inclusive and more effective as we serve our communities.

In this guide, you will find practical ideas for how LGBT organizations can take concrete steps to provide a more welcoming environment for transgender people. We'll address directly the challenges and opportunities that present themselves in this process.

This resource is specifically written for LGBT groups and organizations that want to be more inclusive of transgender people. This will mean various things to different kinds of groups—from welcoming more transgender people on your soccer team to passing transgender-inclusive legislation to running transgender-specific programs at your community center. We encourage you to take the ideas in this guide and think of ways in which you can apply them to your unique organization and mission.

LGBT organizations are made up of a wide range of people, including family, friends, and allies. Our volunteers, staffs and constituencies identify as lesbian, bisexual, straight, gay, transgender, non-transgender, queer and more. When we refer to LGBT organizations in this guide, it is our intention to speak to this diverse group of people with the goal of helping our community become increasingly inclusive.

Other organizations that are not LGBT-specific in their focus may also find this guide helpful. Please feel free to translate the information from the LGBT experience to your own in ways that are useful to you.

TRANSGENDER INCLUSION

Transgender people have been a part of the LGBT movement from its beginnings. As people began to see their sexual orientation as a healthy part of their identity, and found the prejudice they faced oppressive, they found common cause with those who expressed their gender differently than the majority of society. Together, they began the work that we continue—striving to create a world where we are free to be ourselves and where our identities are never a justification for discrimination and violence.

Those who oppose our rights see LGBT people as a common community. We are targeted for stigmatization and violence together as a group because we break stereotypes. Our common vulnerabilities may have brought us together, but the LGBT community works together because we are working towards a common purpose, for the freedom to be who we are and the right to live with dignity and justice.

When we talk about transgender-inclusion in this guide, it is with the understanding that transgender people are inherently a part of the LGBT community and have been from the beginning. In some ways, the term "transgender-inclusion" is not perfect; it could be taken to mean that transgender people aren't inherently a part of something called the LGB(T) movement and that instead, transgender people have been added to the LGB movement. We use this term, despite this perceived limitation, because we believe it is the best term to describe the process of integration of transgender people throughout one's LGBT organization and it is the term that our movement has been using for over a decade.

We also realize that the term "LGBT" sometimes glosses over the gap that exists between the realities of our community organizations (that they are not always inclusive) and the diverse and vast world of LGBT people. We know that our organizations want to accurately reflect and meaningfully serve LGBT people. Working together can be challenging and we need to be intentional in order to create a truly diverse and vibrant community.

As Suzanne Pharr has noted in her ground-breaking book, *Homophobia: A Weapon of Sexism,* homophobia is driven by a rigid gender code. A long-time feminist, Pharr observed that women who break out of constricting gender roles and take leadership in their communities are often branded as "lesbian" to make them stop pushing for change—whether that change means better schools for their children, clean-up of a toxic waste dump, or marriage equality. Similarly, men who visibly challenge gender conformity—by confronting male violence, expressing emotion, or embracing their artistic or "feminine" sides—are punished both socially and in the world of work. Simply, gender bias and homophobia are inextricably entwined.

Gay, lesbian and bisexual people have often constituted a significant share of our society's gender outlaws, standing side by side on the gender non-conforming continuum with our transgender peers and bearing the consequences of not matching the gender stereotypes of straight society. Accordingly, bias against gender non-conformity threatens access to employment and other key societal institutions for all of us and exposes us to violence and prejudice. While we may not all be in the exact same boat, we are certainly all in the same water.

The divisive and disappointing federal legislative battle around the removal of gender identity/expression protections from the Employment Non-Discrimination Act in 2007 should not confuse any of us. There is no secure equality for LGB people without protections for gender bias. On a parallel course, there is no true community and no authentic expression of queer life or culture without transgender people. Often the most stigmatized people in our ranks, gender non-conforming people have consistently led the charge for change in our movement and the society at large. We marginalize them/us at our own peril.

In different times and in different places, the LGBT community has varied between close-knit cohesion and an uneasy alliance between lesbian, gay, bisexual and transgender activists. We have been divided along lines of gender, gender identity/expression, race, class, abilities and more. But we believe that at the heart of the LGBT movement is a passion for inclusion and that at our best, and most effective, the LGBT community strives to open our doors to all who want to work together with people of all sexual orientations and gender identities and expressions.

We hope this book provides you with the concrete tools you need to fully realize your vision for a fully transgender-inclusive organization. There is so much work to do and so many challenges facing our movement. We must draw on the vast talents and strengths that our brilliant, diverse communities have to offer to achieve our goal of full equality.

OPENING THE DOOR TO A TRANSGENDER-INCLUSIVE MOVEMENT

The question before us now is not whether transgender people are part of our movement, but rather how to build organizations in which the participation of transgender people is affirming for both them and for the groups to which they belong. The purpose of this guide is to consider how we can strengthen that partnership so that the political and social organizations that we have worked so hard to build can truly be as diverse, effective and inclusive as we want them to be.

THE CHALLENGES WE FACE

One of the most significant challenges LGBT organizations face is that transgender (and bisexual) labels have often been added in name (the addition of the "B" and "T" to LGBT) without any authentic effort to integrate transgender and bisexual people and experiences into the organization. While often well-intentioned, changes in name only render the impact of adding those letters almost meaningless, as transgender people have learned the hard way. Because the addition of the "T" only sometimes translates into concrete programs or even a genuine welcome, trans people may view the "T" with suspicion or simply ignore it altogether.

Transgender people have also encountered overt hostility in some LGBT organizations. Some people—regardless of their sexual orientation—are uncomfortable with transgender people because of the transphobia that they have learned from the larger society. Sometimes lesbian and gay people recycle the homophobia they have heard and use it against transgender people, saying things like, "that's not natural," or "it's just a phase." Not intending to be hostile, some LGB people have pointed out the real differences between being LGB and T, and the different ways in which people experience discrimination, and have said that their organization should treat these issues differently. Whatever the reasoning, the result is that transgender people have learned, through painful experience, that lesbian, gay and bisexual spaces are not always welcoming, safe environments for them. Using prejudice to exclude others based on their identity weakens our movement and, as leaders, we must take whatever steps we can to counteract it.

Sometimes, gay, lesbian and bisexual people genuinely want to welcome transgender people but don't know how. We may inadvertently include people in a way that demonstrates ignorance of the issues of gender identity/expression. For example, we might write a newsletter article on "LGBT marriage issues," failing to recognize that marriage rights for transgender people pose a different set of questions than same-sex marriage rights for non-transgender people. Or we might ask people if they are gay, lesbian, bisexual or transgender, rather than seeing that a person can be lesbian, gay, or bisexual and transgender.

THE JOURNEY TO A TRANS-INCLUSIVE LGBT ORGANIZATION

Although the path of each LGBT organization towards full trans-inclusion is different, there are some common stages. Different organizations spend different amounts of time in each stage and may experience these in a different order. This not always a linear process but we hope to show the ways in which organizations change over time as they become more inclusive. It is helpful to examine these different stages to see that LGBT organizations do face similar challenges to trans-inclusion and learn how other organizations have moved through the process of becoming fully transgender-inclusive.

STAGE ONE: NOT ON THE RADAR

Organizations in this stage have not yet recognized that they have an exclusionary posture and practice regarding transgender people. They typically don't have a "T" in their name and have not developed their mission statements to involve, serve or celebrate transgender people. They have no out transgender people on their staff or board; they make no attempt to serve trans people or make their facilities or events trans-affirming or -accessible. There are no policies to address transphobia or harassment, so jokes about gender non-conforming people, if they occur, go unchallenged. The organization makes no alliances with organizations that serve or advocate for the rights of trans people.

STAGE TWO: NOT IN THE MISSION, BUT TRANS PEOPLE ARE WELCOME

Leaders and members of these organizations may be personally welcoming of transgender people, but the organization itself still has a mission that only mentions sexual orientation or LGB people. People running these organizations may say they are not sure how to be trans-inclusive, since they may believe they don't know any transgender people. They may believe that there is no need to be trans-inclusive because they are not aware whether an active transgender community even exists in the area. In this stage, individuals in the organization or on the board may challenge anti-transgender attitudes, but there is no organizational commitment to addressing this systematically, and no larger trans-affirming policy work.

STAGE THREE: A TRANS-INCLUSIVE MISSION AND POSSIBLY THE BEGINNINGS OF TRANS-INCLUSIVE PROGRAMMING AND/OR ADVOCACY

An organization in this stage has either incorporated transgender people in their mission or they were founded with a trans-inclusive mission originally. However, their trans-inclusion may be mostly on paper. In many ways, the "ethic" of the LGBT movement has evolved so that there is now an expectation that groups have a "T" in their name, and this may have been the motivation for developing a trans-inclusive mission. Yet, the actual activities of the organization may not have caught up to the change in mission, leaving transgender people to have negative or mixed experiences with staff or at events.

An organization in this stage may also be doing some things to realize their mission, such as ensuring that educational events/programs include transgender people as speakers, posting event notices on transgender list serves, and using the term LGBT instead of LGB. But while transgender people are invited to participate, there is no effort to recruit trans people into leadership positions.

STAGE FOUR: THE ORGANIZATION'S WORK IS TRANS-INCLUSIVE AND THERE IS GREATER TRANS INVOLVEMENT THROUGHOUT THE ORGANIZATION

Organizations in this stage have missions that are trans-inclusive and they take this seriously.

The work of the organization reflects the needs of LGB and T people most of the time, and there are transgender people at most levels of the organization, from volunteers to board members. In terms of its policy work, organizations at stage four commit to policy work that is fully inclusive of transgender rights and concerns.

This stage includes organizations that sometimes do things that are not fully trans-inclusive.

Their name may not be trans-inclusive, they may not have fixed all of the physical space issues that block trans people from fully participating, or there are some people affiliated with the organization who are not fully on board with trans-inclusion or don't know how to be.

Nonetheless, there is an institution-wide commitment to understanding and addressing the needs of transgender people. Anti-trans jokes and attitudes are confronted and challenged.

Transgender people feel positive accessing services and coming to events. Trans people on staff have access to the same advancement opportunities as their LGB peers.

STAGE FIVE: THE FULLY-INCLUSIVE ORGANIZATION THAT PRIORITIZES TRANSGENDER WORK

The fully transgender-inclusive organization has trans people involved at all levels and the activities of the organization always reflect the needs of transgender people as well as LGB people. Safe, accessible bathrooms are the norm. Organizations at this stage recognize that there are some activities that need to be done specifically to meet the needs of trans people and it is an organizational priority to get these things done. For example, a political advocacy organization at this stage would be actively working on ensuring that transgender people can get driver's licenses and other documents that reflect the gender they live as, in addition to the other legislative priorities of the organization (such as relationship recognition bills).

At a stage five organization, there is a recognition and true culture of celebration around the vibrant legacy of transgender leadership in the LGBT movement. Transgender leadership is seen as bringing essential talents and perspectives to any effort undertaken.

ACTION IDEAS FOR LGBT GROUPS

Throughout this guide, we've been talking about actions for a wide variety of LGBT groups. However, given the broad diversity of LGBT organizations, clubs and events, there are some actions that need to be addressed by specific types of groups. Here are some ideas to get you started:

POLITICAL/ADVOCACY GROUPS

- Ensure that all proactive bills/policies you support include sexual orientation and gender identity or expression
- If policies or laws exist that only include sexual orientation, work to get gender identity/expression protections added
- Prioritize working on transgender-specific policy needs, such as fighting for driver's license policies that allow transgender people to change gender markers, or fighting for transgender healthcare to be covered through public and private health insurance
- Insist that legislators and other elected officials say "lesbian, gay, bisexual and transgender" instead of "gay" or "gay and lesbian"

- If you ask candidates running for office their stances on LGBT issues, include transgender policy priorities in the questions and then only endorse candidates who are fully supportive of transgender rights
- Invite transgender non-political groups to provide input on what advocacy or political needs they have, by inviting them to forums or by meeting with them directly
- Insist that the local or state government has trans-gender-inclusive policies throughout, such as training police and emergency personnel to be trans-sensitive
- Ensure that transgender people are sent to meetings with legislators so that legislators see that the "T" is a true part of the organization and priorities

COMMUNITY CENTERS

- Host support groups or social events for transgender people of all varieties, such as for men, women, gen-derqueer people, cross-dressers, etc.
- Ensure that men's and women's groups allow trans-gender men and women respectively
- Generally ensure that all programs are trans-inclu-sive, and find ways to indicate trans-inclusiveness in advertisements/descriptions for all programs/events
- If relevant, find ways to increase security outside of the center building to prevent anti-transgender vio-lence. Have volunteers or others stand outside the building when people are arriving for events to deter harassment or violence
- If there is an incident of anti-transgender violence in the community, ensure that your community center

becomes the response center where people can go to plan actions and get needed help

- In libraries, include books, videos, and DVD's on transgender topics
- Maintain referral lists of providers and groups (medical, social, etc.) geared for transgender people
- Provide gender-neutral restrooms
- Declare one room in the center to be a changing room

HEALTH ORGANIZATIONS

- Create a referral list to transgender-affirming medical and mental health providers and a network of medical and mental health providers
- Train staff to be sensitive and supportive of transgender care issues
- Use forms that recognize transgender individuals and their specific health care situation
- Provide a safe space for patients to receive transgender-specific health care, including hormones, gynecological care, etc.
- Be sure that HIV prevention and treatment information includes the needs and perspectives of transgender people
- Recognize that the names that patients/clients use may be different than that known or used by their insurance carrier; use the person's chosen name and pronouns when speaking with the person and when calling them when in the waiting room
- Advocate, as needed, with insurance companies for appropriate care (for example, pap smears for female-to-male patients is routinely turned down by insurance

companies; you may need to explain that this is necessary care and not a billing error on your part)

- Realize that some transgender people (and others) have difficulty revealing their bodies or disclosing their transgender identity; provide a safe space that treats the patient with respect and understanding
- Many transgender people have had negative experiences with health care providers, leaving them feeling stigmatized or wary. Acknowledge, as appropriate, and work through these issues to establish a positive relationship with the client/patient

CAMPUS ORGANIZATIONS

- Get your university to add "gender identity or expression" to its nondiscrimination policy
- Fight for more gender-neutral bathrooms on campus (single- and multi-use)
- Work for gender-neutral dorms, or, ensure that transgender students can choose their roommate or be assured to be housed with a transgender-friendly roommate
- Bring a trans speaker to campus as part of your LGBT Awareness Week/Month
- Hold a Transgender Awareness Week with a variety of trans-related programming
- Ensure that students and alumni can update their records with their new gender and names
- Ensure that trans students can get their needs met at the student health center and counseling centers and that trans-related services and counseling are covered by student health insurance

- Train critical personnel on campus on trans sensitivity (and, ideally, all staff). Critical personnel include: public safety officers, resident advisors, student health center staff, counselors. Include how to respond to anti-transgender harassment and violence
- Bring up transgender issues in classroom discussions or recommend to professors how to add issues to syllabi
- Set up internship programs with local, state, and national LGBT and transgender organizations

CONCLUSION

By now you have a very good idea of what it is going to take to move your LGBT organization along in its journey to become fully transgender-inclusive. If you have a long way to go, you may feel overwhelmed. Rest assured, by slowly taking steps one by one, you will get where you need to go, and bring along the others in your organization with you. Many hands make light work. You will likely find the process enlightening and empowering. It certainly has been for us in our work in building transgender-inclusive LGBT organizations.

The work of trans-inclusion is critically important. Have no doubt that each of us doing our part will create a new world where it is safe and acceptable to identify as any gender and express our gender in any form we choose. As LGBT organizations demonstrate trans-inclusion, our example will be noted by other organizations and institutions we work with; indeed, we should be actively encouraging them to adopt these practices. Ultimately, our hope is that through each of us making our part of the world trans-inclusive, we will help spread trans-friendly attitudes and behaviors everywhere.

As Mahatma Gandhi said, "You must be the change you wish to see in the world." The power to change the world is yours and ours; we must recognize that power and use it to create a dynamic, inclusive LGBT movement. Hopefully, this guide will support that process. We look forward to working with you and your organization as we build an ever stronger, more powerful, and fully integrated movement for justice.

1. Why might lesbian, gay, and bisexual advocacy organizations need this guide to become more transgender inclusive?

CHAPTER 5

WHAT THE MEDIA SAY

The question of gender identity has garnered more and more interest in the media in recent years. Transgender characters in popular TV shows have exposed a large number of people to a subject matter they might otherwise not have come in contact with, and the stories of celebrities transitioning have been discussed widely and controversially. Some believe the increased visibility of non-conforming gender identity—for a long time too taboo to be explored—is a symptom of increasing acceptance, and a sign that society has reached a tipping point in regard to its treatment of these individuals. Not all stories are positive, though, and while this social movement has made progress, the media have to report ongoing problems as well. Different media outlets can report on issues of gender identity in different ways: while some can give a voice to transgender people who are otherwise unrepresented, some give a platform to those who are critical of the movement for transgender rights.

"AMERICA HAS NOT REACHED A TRANSGENDER TIPPING POINT," BY ERIC SASSON, FROM THE *NEW REPUBLIC*, APRIL 27, 2015

Without a doubt, it was an extraordinary week for the transgender community. Model Andreja Pejic made history by becoming the first transgender woman to be profiled in *Vogue*. Laverne Cox, Emmy nominee for "Orange Is the New Black," joined several other women baring it all for *Allure*'s annual "Nudes" issue, becoming the first transgender actress to do so. And of course, there was Diane Sawyer's highly-rated interview with Bruce Jenner, which, as other outlets have pointed out, was notable mainly for what Sawyer did not do (and which past interviewers have done): fixate on Jenner's genitals and any decisions regarding future surgery; conflate gender and sexual orientation; or sensationalize the episode with inappropriate pictures or invasive questions. Sawyer mostly let Jenner speak for himself, even asking Jenner what pronoun he prefers (which explains my use of "himself" and "he" in this sentence).

And yet, one wonders if the media is engaging in a bit too much self-congratulation for the apparent "progress" that transgender people have made. Outlets fell over themselves to herald Cox's "groundbreaking" shoot and praise her "flawless" figure. CNN called the Jenner interview "America's transgender moment," while *Time* speculated that it could be a "watershed moment." This, after *Time* cover story on Cox last year on how America is reaching a "transgender tipping point," a phrase *Vogue* lifted verbatim for the headline of its feature on Pejic.

But if America is reaching a turning point on transgender issues, so far it is strictly in terms of visibility—not, as one might hope, in terms of America's overall attitudes and laws.

Not that visibility isn't important. Gay and lesbian visibility, i.e., the willingness for more people in the public sphere to come out, was arguably the most important catalyst in advancing gay rights in our country. And while we still have a long way to go to eradicate homophobia, at least the laws and the polls are moving in the right direction. With 37 states implementing marriage equality— the Supreme Court is set to rule on constitutionality this June—and a slew of polling showing attitudes towards gay and lesbians have shifted demonstrably, progress is no longer measured by the Ellens and Eltons and Neil-Patricks we see in the news, but by the girl in Arkansas who gets to take her girlfriend to the prom or a man marrying his partner in Oklahoma.

As such, we ought to be careful not to oversell the "progress" we are seeing on transgender issues, remembering that the visibility of a select few rich, famous, and/ or beautiful people may not reflect the reality experienced by the transgender community as a whole.

For that reality, according to statistics provided by the National Gay and Lesbian Task Force's largest survey on the transgender community, is not just sobering, but downright depressing. Sawyer touched upon this in her interview, referring to the high suicide rates among the transgender population and the lack of workplace protection in all but a few handful of states. This barely scratches the surface of the struggles that the vast majority of transgender people face: 90 percent of those surveyed reported experiencing harassment, mistreatment or discrimination on the job, and 47 percent said they were fired, not hired or denied a promotion because of being transgender or gender non-conforming. Nineteen percent have experienced homelessness at some point in their lives. Transgender youth in grades K-12 reported alarming rates of harassment (78 percent), physical assault (35 percent) and sexual violence (12 percent). For transgender people of color, poverty rates over eight times the national average; HIV infection rates are over 20 percent, compared to 2.4 percent for the general black population; and almost half have attempted suicide.

And yet, these statistics shouldn't surprise us once we examine the abysmal state of transgender rights in America. The majority of states in the United States do not have laws prohibiting discrimination in employment based on gender identity/expression, nor do they have anti-bullying or anti-discrimination laws to protect students, or hate crime laws specifically designed to protect people in this class. Only eight states provide any form of transition-related insurance, while 20 states still have "unclear or burdensome" requirements for transgender people to change their identities. And if that's not enough, several states have recently attempted to pass laws requiring individuals to use bathrooms based on their "biological birth" gender.

This is not to say that highlighting these positive steps is wrong. The tendency for media outlets to celebrate these moments is admirable; one hopes that they will inspire those who are transgender and suffering to see change on the horizon and empower them to be part of that change. But much as racism hardly ended with the election of Obama, transphobia is not going away anytime soon. In fact, it's rearing its ugly head so often that we need to remind ourselves to place this week's positive news in the greater context of the struggle for transgender acceptance and dignity. For every Laverne Cox, there are still far too many Leelah Alcorns.

1. Do you agree or disagree with the author's position that the state of transgender rights is "abysmal" in the United States? How much progress does society have to make for transgender people to be fully accepted?

2. Leelah Alcorns was a trans woman who committed suicide due, in part, to the inability of those close to her to accept her gender identity. Do you think the media gives enough attention to the plights of trans people such as Leelah?

"THE OPERATION THAT CAN RUIN YOUR LIFE," JULIE BINDEL, FROM *STANDPOINT MAGAZINE*, NOVEMBER 2009

Last year, I was nominated for the Stonewall Journalist of the Year award. This seemed fair enough since I write prolifically about sexuality and sexual identity. But I guessed that Stonewall would not dare give me the prize, because a powerful lobby affiliated with the lesbian and gay communities had been hounding me for five years. Six weeks later I, along with a police escort, walked past a huge demonstration of transsexuals and their supporters, shouting "Bindel the Bigot." Despite campaigning against gender discrimination, rape, child abuse and domestic violence for 30 years, I have been labelled a bigot because of a column I wrote in 2004 that questioned whether a sex change would make someone a woman or simply a man without a penis. Subsequently, I was "no platformed" by the National Union of Students Women's Campaign, a privilege previously afforded to fascist groups such as the BNP. As a leading feminist writer, I now find that a number of organisations are too frightened to ask me to speak at public events for fear of protests by transsexual lobbyists.

The 2004 column was about a Canadian male-to-female transsexual who had taken a rape crisis centre to court over its decision not to invite her to be a counsellor for rape victims. Feminists tend to be critical of traditional gender roles because they benefit men and oppress women. Transsexualism, by its nature, promotes the idea that it is "natural" for boys to play with guns and girls to play with Barbie dolls. The idea that gender roles are biologically determined rather than socially constructed is the antithesis of feminism.

I wrote: "Those who 'transition' seem to become stereotypical in their appearance — f**k-me shoes and birds' nest hair for the boys; beards, muscles and tattoos for the girls. Think about a world inhabited just by trans-sexuals. It would look like the set of *Grease*."

Gender dysphoria (GD) was invented in the 1950s by reactionary male psychiatrists in an era when men were men and women were doormats. It is a term used to describe someone who feels strongly that they should belong to the opposite sex and that they were born in the wrong body. GD has no proven genetic or physiological basis.

A review for the *Guardian* in 2005 of more than 100 international medical studies of post-operative trans-sexuals by the University of Birmingham's Aggressive Research Intelligence Facility found no robust scientific evidence that gender reassignment surgery was clinically effective. It warned that the results of many gender reas-signment studies were unsound because researchers lost track of more than half of the participants.

The past decade has seen an increase in the number of people diagnosed as transsexual. There are now 1,500-1,600 new referrals a year to one of the handful of gender identity clinics in Britain. About 1,200 receive treatment on the NHS with the rest going private, Thailand being the main country of choice. The largest clinic, at Charing Cross Hospital in London, saw 780 new referrals last year. The NHS carried out some 150 operations in the last year (up from about 100 in 2005-2006). Apart from Thailand, the country with the highest number of sex-change operations is Iran where, homosexuality is illegal and punishable by death. When sex-change surgery is performed on gay men, they become, in the eyes of the gender defenders, heterosexual women. Transsexual surgery becomes modern-day aversion therapy for gays and lesbians.

In the West, however, supporting the diagnosis and availability of surgical intervention is seen as a view right-thinking liberals should adopt. But no oppressed group ever insisted its emotional distress was the sole basis for the establishment of a right. Indeed, transsexuals, along with those seeking IVF and cosmetic surgery, are using the NHS for the pursuit of happiness not health.

Treatment is brutal and the results far from perfect. Male-to-female surgery involves removal of the penis and scrotum and the construction of a "vagina" using the skin from the phallus, breast implants inserted and the trachea shaved. Painful laser treatment to remove hair in the beard area and elsewhere and cosmetic surgery to "feminise" the face is increasingly common.

For female-to-male surgery, breasts, womb and ovaries are removed. Testosterone injections, usually prescribed shortly after the initial diagnosis, result in the growth of facial hair and deepening of the voice.

Recent legislation (the Gender Recognition Act, which allows people to change sex and be issued with a new birth certificate) will have a profoundly negative effect on the human rights of women and children. Since 2004, it has been possible for those diagnosed with GD to be assigned the sex of their choice, providing that the person has lived as the opposite sex for two years, has no plans to change back again and can provide evidence of the above.

It is not necessary to have undergone hormone treatment or surgery. In other words, a pre-operative man could apply for a job in a women-only rape counselling service and, if refused on grounds of his sex, could take the employer to court on the grounds that "he" is legally a "she."

A definition of transsexualism used by a number of transsexual rights organisations reads:

> Students who are gender non-conforming are those whose gender expression (or outward appearance) does not follow traditional gender roles: "feminine boys," "masculine girls" and students who are androgynous, for example. It can also include students who look the way boys and girls are expected to look but participate in activities that are gender nonconforming, like a boy who does ballet. The term "transgender youth" can be used as an umbrella term for all students whose gender identity is different from the sex they were assigned at birth and/or whose gender expression is non-stereotypical.

According to this definition, a girl who plays football is transsexual.

A number of transsexuals are beginning to admit that opting for surgery ruined their lives. "I was a messed-up young gay man," says Claudia McClean, a male-to-female transsexual who opted for surgery 20 years ago. "If I had been offered an alternative to a sex change, I would have jumped at the chance." A number of transsexuals I have spoken to tell me how easy it is to be referred for surgery if they trot out a cliche such as, "I felt trapped in the wrong body."

Transsexualism is becoming so normalised that increasing numbers of children are being referred to clinics by their parents. Recently, an 18-month-old baby in Denmark was diagnosed as suffering from GD. Last summer, a primary school headteacher held an assembly to explain that a nine-year-old boy would return as a girl.

Ten years ago, there were an average of six child and adolescent referrals per year in Britain, but in 2008 numbers had increased six-fold. Although the minimum age for sex-change surgery is 18, puberty-blocking hormones can be prescribed to those as young as 16, and transsexual rights lobbyists want that age to be reduced to 13.

James Bellringer is a surgeon at Charing Cross Hospital, which has the largest gender identity clinic in the UK. He believes that children should be allowed to self-diagnose as GD. "It is not the doctors saying, 'You are a transsexual, let's get you on hormones,' it is the children saying, 'I don't like my breasts, I feel like a girl.'"

There is, however, a dispute within the medical profession about whether puberty-blockers should be prescribed. Some doctors say that children need to expe-rience puberty to know whether they are misplaced in their bodies. I would describe preventing puberty as a modern form of child abuse. Two-thirds of those claiming to be, or diagnosed as, transsexual during childhood become lesbian or gay in later life. "I would be happy living now as a gay man, comfortable in the body I was born with," says McClean. "The prejudice against me for being an effem-inate boy who fancied other boys was too much to bear. Changing sex meant I could be normal."

Medical science cannot turn a biological male into a biological female — it can only alter the appearance of body parts. A transsexual "woman" will always be a biological male. A male-to-female transsexual serving a prison sentence for manslaughter and rape won the right to be relocated to a women's jail. Her lawyers argued that her rights were being violated by being unable to live in her role as a woman in a men's jail. Large numbers of female prisoners have experienced childhood abuse and rape and will fail to appreciate the reasons behind a biological man living among them, particularly one who still has the penis with which he raped a woman. (Some transsexuals choose to retain their genitals.)

There is a handful of radicals in the world today who have dared to challenge the diagnosis of transsexualism. Those who do are called "transphobic" and treated with staggering vitriol. There is a form of cultural relativism at play here. Defenders of female genital mutilation or forced marriage often use the argument that such practices can be justified within certain communities (i.e. non-Western cultures), despite the fact that they serve to dehumanise women, because it is the "truth" of that particular community. After I had been shortlisted for the Stonewall award, scores of blogs and message boards filled with a call to arms against me.

On one, "Genocide and Julie Bindel," a poster wrote, "What would Stonewall's reaction have been had a BME [black and minority ethnic] group nominated Ayatollah Khomeini as Politician of the Year? She is an active oppressor of trans people. I hope she dies an agonising and premature death of cancer in the very near future. It would make the world a better place."

I had some support, some from those who had also experienced a transsexual-led witchhunt. I heard from post-operative transsexuals who had been railroaded into surgery and now regretted it. "Do not publish my name," said one, "but if anyone questions the validity of sex-change treatment you are sent to Coventry by the 'community' elders."

A police officer who, during the course of his duty, was unfairly accused by transsexuals of "transphobia" was driven to a breakdown by their vicious campaign. An eminent medical ethicist who had dared to defend a fellow professional who had questioned the diagnosis of GD from a scientific point of view almost lost his career and reputation. And several women from feminist organisations have been bullied and vilified for challenging the "right" of male-to-female transsexuals to work in women-only organisations.

Dr Caillean McMahon, a US-based forensic psychiatrist, defines herself not as a transsexual but as a "woman of operative history. The trans community has an unforgiving global sort of condemnation towards critical outsiders. I have to be suspicious that the insistence of many of those demanding to enter it is not for the purpose of celebrating the spirit and nature of women, but to seek an enforced validation, extracted by force in a legal or political manner." With the normalisation of transsexual surgery comes an acceptance of other forms of surgery to correct a mental disorder. In 2000, Russell Reid, a psychiatrist who has diagnosed hundreds of people with GD, was involved in controversy over the condition known as Body Dysmorphic Disorder (BDD), where sufferers can experience a desperate urge to rid themselves of a limb. Reid referred two BDD patients to a surgeon for leg amputations. "When I first heard of people wanting amputations, it seemed bizarre in the extreme," he said in a TV

CRITICAL PERSPECTIVES ON GENDER IDENTITY

documentary. "But then I thought, 'I see transsexuals and they want healthy parts of their body removed in order to adjust to their idealised body image,' and so I think that was the connection for me. I saw that people wanted to have their limbs off with equally as much degree of obsession and need."

In a world where equality between men and women was reality, transsexualism would not exist. The diagnosis of GD needs to be questioned and challenged. We live in a society that, on the whole, respects the human rights of others. Accepting a situation where the surgeon's knife and lifelong hormonal treatment are replacing the acceptance of difference is a scandal. Sex-change surgery is unnecessary mutilation. Using human rights laws to normalise transsexualism has resulted in a backward step in the feminist campaign for gender equality. Perhaps we should give up and become men.

1. Do you agree or disagree with the author's position on transgender people and sex reassignment surgery? Why or why not?

2. Is sex reassignment surgery the right choice for every transgender person? What might be some of its drawbacks?

"US HITS DISTURBING MILESTONE WITH RECORD HIGH NUMBER OF TRANSGENDER MURDERS," BY ANDREW GERMANOS, FROM *COMMON DREAMS*, NOVEMBER 13, 2015

It's been described as a national crisis—yet it's an issue that's rarely the focus of national media attention.

That issue is anti-transgender violence, and a new report out from the Human Rights Campaign (HRC) Foundation and the Trans People of Color Coalition (TPOCC) notes a disturbing record—in 2015, the number of victims of transgender fatal violence in the U.S. hit a record high—21.

There were 13 such murders in 2014, and 19 in 2013. 87 percent of those victims were people of color. The victims, who are disproportionately trans women of color, "are more than alarming statistics. They were human beings with friends and loved ones," the report stresses.

The total toll may even be higher, as the "lack of accurate and reliable data collection makes it impossible for advocates to know how widespread this violence really is."

The report also documents the litany of struggles, abuses, and marginalization transgender people often face, including widespread harassment, sexual assault, partner violence, problems accessing proper healthcare, and denial of safety nets.

"There are now more transgender homicide victims in 2015 than in any other year that advocates have recorded. At least 21 people—nearly all of them transgender women of color—have lost their lives to violence," HRC President Chad Griffin said in a media statement.

"This kind of violence is often motivated by anti-transgender bias; but that is rarely the only factor. At a time when transgender people are finally gaining visibility and activists are forcing our country to confront systemic violence against people of color, transgender women of color are facing an epidemic of violence that occurs at the intersections of racism, sexism and transphobia—issues that advocates can no longer afford to address separately," Griffin stated.

Chase Strangio, a staff attorney with the ACLU's LGBT and AIDS Project, spoke to *Democracy Now!* in August, when the number of transgender women killed in the year totaled 17, and said that the violence against transgender people is "systemic and it is institutional."

"This is a state of emergency for the transgender community. And it's a state of emergency that's disproportionately affecting transgender women of color, and particularly black trans women. And we are living in a moment where we should be incredibly concerned about all of the mechanisms of violence against our community," he said.

The new report was issued just days ahead of Congress' first-ever forum on violence against transgender people.

"This week, as we seek to raise awareness of the issues facing the trans community, it is important to renew our commitment to help trans individuals be free of the fear of violence or bullying just for being who they are," said California Rep. Mike Honda, who is to chair a task force on transgender equality.

"It is my hope that by launching this workforce and holding a first-ever forum, we will reach some of my colleagues and encourage them to stand with the trans community," Honda said. "It is only through social change that we can truly elevate the conversation in this country and reach a place of true understanding and embrace all people for who they are."

1. As this article states, why might the media not be covering violence against transgender individuals?

"7 TRANS MEDIA TROPES THAT NEED TO STOP," BY JAMES ST. JAMES, FROM *EVERYDAY FEMINISM*, FEBRUARY 18, 2015

I totally started writing this before *Transparent* recently won its two Golden Globes, so I'm—like—such a trans hipster right now. Just so you know.

Okay, so **trans narratives have gone supernova lately**, particularly over the last couple of years. They're the new cash cow. Nobody wants a gay best friend anymore; it's all about the trans best friend. The trans parent. The trans prisoner. The trans child.

And that can be really cool in its own way. Coverage and attention can help us, as trans people, continue to break into the mainstream, if only to just say hi. It's nice to know that cis people are starting to notice that we exist. **Recognition of our existence is a great foundational step toward being treated like we're actually human.**

Buuuuut it's not always a basket of roses.

See, because with transness being treated this way, **quite a bit of it is being capitalized on by cis people** (directors, producers, screenwriters, authors, and so on). And with all those cis fingerprints, so many tropes are continuing to spread throughout mainstream media about the trans identity at large.

Trans characters are continuing not to be characters who are trans, but rather mechanisms solely for the benefit of the cis audience through cis characters in a cis plot.

We're being used.

The problem with imposing the cis entertainment palette on trans people is the mainstream still doesn't have a base sense of what or who a trans person is. To put negative, incorrect, or overgeneralizing labels on us just makes cis people think trans people are indeed evil, confused, or only exist to educate cis people about trans lives.

For example...

1. BEING PEGGED AS A DECEIVER, LIAR, OR MENTALLY UNSTABLE INDIVIDUAL

The most iconic example of this trope is the kidnapper and murderer in *Silence of the Lambs,* who forces cis women to rub lotion all over their bodies until it's soft enough to be peeled right off for personal wear. It's where we got the (in)famous phrase, "It rubs the lotion on its skin or else it gets the hose again." Ick.

Trans narratives are also rife with lying and deceiving cis characters, usually by "tricking" them through the accurate representation of their identities.

Note how the so-called tricking is rarely done by the trans person in some intentional, backward way, but rather the mistake of cis assumption by the given cis character, who often is falling in love with them.

But is the cis ignorance still the trans person's fault? Of course it is. Who can forget the big reveal in *The Crying Game?* Audiences couldn't shut the hell up about it for years, conveniently ignoring the lover's mistreatment of the trans character thereafter.

2. BEING USED AS A PAMPHLET

Basically, whenever the trans character is on screen or on the page, the talk often immediately moves to trans stuff.

This is an issue because 1) there's more to a trans person than being trans, 2) not all trans people want some sort of (medical) transition (which is what "trans talk" usually entails), and 3) apparently elephants don't need to be discussed unless one's in the room.

As soon as that trans character is no longer present, the trans topic is immediately dropped and forgotten. In the end, trans topics are only present when the character is.

Cis people are being taught an unfortunate lesson through this persistent trope: that **they have no reason to discuss or reflect upon trans issues themselves.** And since it's the cis culture that's brought trans issues to a head, that's kind of bad behavior to encourage.

Also, for so many narratives in the media focusing on a trans person's transition, we start to forget about the actual person. Cis people start to believe that transition is all that makes a trans person as a trans person. And that sucks.

The fact of the matter is we have way more problems than just transition (...yay?), so let's start putting those on the table, too.

As much as I love *Orange is the New Black*, and as much as I respect the great strides its taken – like featuring a trans woman actually played by a trans woman, featuring a trans woman of color, featuring a trans woman dealing with the prison system, featuring a trans woman who's actually complicated and neither entirely good nor entirely bad – it does have one huge flaw in the trans department.

As of this writing, two seasons of the show are out. And within those two seasons, there's been only one scene in which the trans character doesn't magically invoke trans topics. One.

3. BEING ONLY YOUNG AND WHITE (AND MAGICALLY ABLE TO AFFORD MEDICAL TRANSITION)

There's plenty of identity crossover when it comes to people who are trans, but those that primarily get the limelight are the young and white ones.

Their experiences don't culminate all of the trans experience, especially when further reduced to "just" transition and body dysphoria.

Thankfully, there have been a few examples that have managed to peek through.

One of the people featured in *TransGeneration* was both a person of color and a person of altered hearing. *NoRmal* and *Transparent* both feature people above middle-age. As already mentioned, *Orange is the New*

Black has a person of color. So we're slowly, *slowly* creeping forward on that front.

But then there's the problem of trans characters more often than not magically being able to afford medical transition. That shit's expensive and rarely covered by insurance, however universal it is in scant places.

But the world of media often sidesteps this issue. The character in question frequently has a surgeon parent or has been left with a trust fund or – *shhh* – the issue simply never comes up. How did I not see how lucky we are? Surgery for everyone!

At least there are a few examples of people who can't quite glide on the road to transition.

I Am J by Cris Beam features a character so poor that he doesn't even have his own bedroom. Sleeping on the couch every night kind of makes it hard to hide your true identity from your stunted parents, you know? (Bonus points for him also being biracial!)

And one of the heroines in *Tokyo Godfathers* is dealing with homelessness. Suffice it to say transition is a pipedream right now.

4. THE NON-CONSENSUAL 'REVEAL'

The non-consensual "reveal" is hugely problematic in two ways because 1) it is, indeed, non-consensual, thereby taking all of the trans person's rightful power in the situation and handing it over to the cis person, and 2) it suggests that there's something necessary to reveal, even to people who shouldn't matter.

Even when a character's body history isn't disclosed to coworkers or friends of lovers (or even some friends of the trans character's own), they are often still disclosed to lovers and loved ones in "accidental" ways.

It doesn't matter who you are to us. In the end, **knowing our body history is never your right.**

It's never okay to force it out of us through manipulation or threats or physical violence, go through our personal belongings or information, or get shocked or mad or upset with us over this information when it was ultimately your own cis-washed assumptions about people and gender that are causing you to react this way.

Maybe it never happens in a healthy way on the screen or page because that would give us too much rightful power in the situation.

To willingly and wholeheartedly speak our body histories in fiction would mean we'd all also have to actually talk about them. And in a way that actually focuses on the trans person's wants and needs as opposed to the shock and horror the cis person is feeling over the surprise.

The pilot of *Transparent* unfortunately falls into this general category.

Deciding it wasn't the right time to tell her children, the main character arrives home one day, dressed as herself, only to walk in on one of her grown daughters making out with another woman after they broke into the place because, hey, we need to make that non-consensual reveal happen somehow, right?

"...Dad?" the daughter simply asks when she sees her.

Abrupt end of episode.

5. DYING FOR A CIS PERSON

There are all sorts of people with trans experience who end up dying in movies and books for the benefit of cis gender people.

But seriously, where are the stories where a cis gender person dies for the benefit of a trans person? If you know of examples, please comment them. Because I don't know of a single one.

I highly respect what *Rent* has done for the HIV+ community, as well as the lesbian and gay communities, but when the production's trans character died of AIDS complications, *Rent* fell victim to this trope.

By dying, this character somehow comes back in a dream to save one of the cis characters. And then the cis one lives and everybody's all touched by the trans character's selflessness, and the story is over.

Trans people are not simply mechanisms for cis lives. We are not step stools that can be used so you can reach up that much higher.

To suddenly have us switched around in fiction so that we're your devoted pets is nothing short of insulting, especially when juxtaposed to reality. On the whole, your kind has been quite barbaric to my kind. You've stolen many of our lives. Why would we hand over even more of them in fiction?

6. DYING FOR TRANS MARTYRDOM

Stories such as *Rent* often use death as a way to gain trans sympathy from cis audiences. I mean, take *Boys Don't Cry.*

I know this was based on a true story (and some people argue it was about a butch lesbian, not a trans man), but the movie version was definitely sensationalized. Firstly, because **gender non-conforming people are easy to profit off of in our cis-centric society.** Secondly, **it perpetuates that ugly one-two punch of violence against a trans person as a trans person's only redeeming quality.**

The fact of the matter is that we shouldn't need to somehow earn your respect (nay, your mere attention) by dying. You shouldn't only care about us, however momentarily, once we're dead.

We should be hailed as the badasses we are while we're still alive, not just pitied for having been brought down yet-again by the hands of the Almighty Cis.

7. DYING IN GENERAL

The death in *Albert Nobbs* will always stick in my mind as the most bewildering.

The main character gets in the middle of a scuffle, is pushed against the wall at an awkward angle, staggers back to bed, and dies alone in the middle of the night.

Like virtually all trans-related deaths, it was just so unnecessary. We get enough of that in reality. Does our fiction have to be chock full of it, too?

Albert Nobbs dares to take it even further, playing into the sub-trope of being screwed over by cis people even after death. When the usual nonconsensual reveal is had, the main character's life savings is all stolen by a greedy coworker who never cared much for Nobbs anyway.

And that's how the movie ends. Seriously. That's how it ends.

With our lives having been hard enough in reality, can't we at least rest in freaking peace when it comes to fiction?

THE SUPER DUPER TEST OF TRANS AWESOMENESS

You've heard of the Bechdel/Wallace Test, right? the Vito Russo Test? the Finkbeiner Test? Anyway, I present to you my own humble invention: The Super Duper Test of Trans Awesomeness.

Here's how I feel we should analyze a trans character to see whether or not they're actually being used for trans representation, or just plain being used.

The more points one accomplishes, the better off they are. If they actually get all eleven, they're super duper! Whoosh!

To pass The Super Duper Test of Trans Awesomeness, a given piece of media must have the following:

At least one trans character who

- Transcends the white/young/rich embodiment and
- Is in control of their own trans experience and
- Has their own backstory and present narrative that
- Doesn't exist simply to drive the plot for the cis characters or
- Exist merely to capitalize on the popularity of trans narratives or
- Focus only on the trans person's transness, and instead
- Is painted in a light that is neither purely good nor bad, and either
- Doesn't actually die by the end or
- Dies in a way that isn't to heroically save cis people, but

- Nonetheless dies in a way that has a significant effect on the remainder of the plot.

"But dear, deluded James!" you cry out. "That is simply too much criteria! How could somebody possibly ever pass your awful, awful test with all of these demands?! What kind of trans character could we ever be left to write about?!"

...How about a real one?

1. How are trans people typically represented in the media?

2. How does the author suggest transgender people can be better represented in the media?

CHAPTER 6

WHAT ORDINARY
PEOPLE SAY

The number of transgender individuals is relatively small and, as a consequence, many people only know about the topic from the media, from stories about transgender celebrities, or from political discussion. Hence the question of gender identity can feel far removed from cisgender peoples' own lives. For many people, the movement for transgender rights does not affect them and it can be difficult to comprehend that a person may not identify with the gender they were assigned at birth. One should not forget the importance of this movement in the lives of ordinary people, both those who are transgender themselves and those who know and love a transgender person. While those who are transgender obviously face the greatest difficulties, it can also be difficult for cisgender people to deal with transgender people due to their own preconceived ideas and beliefs. In this chapter, transgender activists and ordinary people air their beliefs about gender identity.

"I KNEW I WAS A GIRL AT 8: TRANSITIONING AND TEENAGE ACTIVISM," BY ELI ERLICK, FROM *AUTOSTRADDLE*, SEPTEMBER 30, 2013 (UPDATED VERSION)

I didn't always know I was different from the other kids. There is a common misconception that trans youth have a lifelong knowledge of their gender and must happily present in ways that conform. This isn't true. Despite coming out at the age of eight, I identified strongly with masculinity until realizing I was a girl.

As a young child, I played with toy cars, loved "masculine" colors, and had a respectable action figure collection. I enjoyed each of these, not tying them to a gendered experience. However, when I announced to my class that I was a girl in the third grade, everything changed.

Not only was I the first openly trans youth in my rural county, I was the first openly trans person. My classmates were quick to police my expression. "If you *want* to be a girl, you can't play with trucks!" my eight-year-old friends repeated to me. I had to perform within the lines of a very specific femininity or face even more misgendering and delegitimization. The policing of gender nonconforming children's expressions, needs, and desires is magnified when you're trans. It was deeply disheartening when I learned I couldn't play trading card games, watch certain shows, or dress how I wanted to.

The constant bullying of gender dictation made me feel the need to force myself to enjoy bright colors for clothes and dolls for toys. In retrospect, they weren't things I fundamentally liked outside of being gendered correctly. Even with recognition of my own queerness in my teen years, I continued to lie to friends and family about the innate nature of my gender expression. The pressure to assimilate to gender conformity far outweighed my own internal desires, as it does for many trans people. It took years of unlearning and frustration at coercive gender conformity to finally move away from these desires. It is a privilege and a necessity.

In elementary school, I started to wear dresses and makeup every day. I'd pack clothing from the girl's clothing section in with my books to put on in the classroom when no one was looking. I knew if my parents caught me, I'd have to give them up. After weeks of making it clear I was a girl at school, my teacher gave my Mom and Dad a call.

Despite my protests, the three agreed that this would just end up a phase, and decided to send me to therapy to try and stop me from expressing my true gender. This didn't work out exactly as they planned: instead of following the therapist's instructions to look at myself in the mirror and say that I'm a boy, I used that time to practice putting on my sister's stolen makeup.

My mom, a well-educated doctor, continued to research the topic of transgender children. Unfortunately, this was 2003. The only (seemingly) dependable research was from Kenneth J. Zucker, a self-proclaimed trans "reparative" therapist. His methodologically flawed research purported that an incredibly low number of gender nonconforming children ended up being transgender. The

161

distorted report affirmed my parents' hope that I would change my mind about being a girl. They showed me the study and explained to me what it meant. For years, I tried to tell myself that this was a phase and I would get to live happily as a boy when I got older. Of course, that never happened. This misleading research alongside the perpetual harassing and discrimination in school left me deeply questioning myself.

My school and social life quickly deteriorated. I had a difficult time making friends. The boys didn't like me because I was a girl, the girls didn't like me because I was a boy, and for the few new friends that I could find, their parents refused to let me speak to them outside of school fearing I would infect their children with whatever was wrong with me.

I missed classes and recess because I feared for my safety and was terrified of the isolation. Even the teachers encouraged the other children to tease me for my identity and cheered on their behavior. I was attacked multiple times throughout these years for existing as a gender nonconforming body. I couldn't comprehend why everybody singled me out and why no one would do anything about it.

By age 10 I became quiet and fearful. My family jokingly referred to me as the "shadow child" because of how shy I had become. I stopped wearing skirts and dresses to school, sick of the teasing. As much as I tried to educate the school, very few listened. I believed I was the only person in the world like this and something was wrong with me mentally, as my parents and teachers had been repeating to me. That year, I also had to quit my gymnastics class because the teacher refused to let me participate on the girl's team after eliminating the co-ed group. I distinctly remember the trophies we received for our final performance. The girls had trophies with a woman gymnast on the top and the boys had trophies with men. To my horror, my teacher decided to give me a male trophy, outing me to all the parents that knew me as a girl and subjecting me to more harassment.

The next two years I continued hiding and lying about myself. I was only able to live as a girl part-time. In middle school English class, we learned about Latin roots. One day, a particular word that caught my eye: *trans – across, beyond, through*. I wondered to myself, "Could *transgender* be a word?" I quickly looked it up. I thought I was being creative but the word already had a meaning. I knew transitioning was possible but I didn't know someone under the age of 40 could do it. Now I suddenly had access to thousands of incredible articles, research papers, and success stories. I smiled through the entire week, something rare at that point in my life. I became fascinated with trans people, wanting to someday become completely open about being one. Unlike many, I had no desire to drop out of the community but to simply live as my authentic self: a trans woman.

Despite being enlightened on trans issues, my junior high school life still wasn't a happy period. There was a large eighth grade graduation ceremony every year and the graduating students had to wear very gendered clothes and were separated on the stage by their gender. All this was in front of a crowd of a few hundred community members. I couldn't go through with that. I had planned months ahead to leave an *I Think I Might Be Transgender: Now What Do I Do?* pamphlet on my parents' bedside table before the ceremony. I hoped they would understand the message and spare me from going.

When the night of my plan finally came, I couldn't sleep. I hoped to wake up in the morning to acceptance. Instead, they said nothing and I was too frightened to ask them about it.

The dreaded graduation ceremony finally rolled around. My heart beat with sorrow as I walked into the community center in "men's" dress pants and a polo shirt.

"Eli you look so handsome! I guess you were a boy all along," said a voice behind me. I didn't want to turn around. Instead, I ran outside and cried. I could hear comments from teachers and family friends about my appearance. I didn't know what I was supposed to do. I let my parents push me back inside. On the stage, I scooted my chair back, trying to conceal myself from the audience. I just closed my eyes and hoped the whole thing would end. Only after an hour of hiding behind my classmates could I finally leave. Some of my parents' friends told them I should see a therapist. They didn't realize what was really wrong. On our way back to the car, my frustrated dad asked, "Is this about you being transgender?" I looked away, ashamed.

However at this point in my life, my parents began to accept my gender identity. My mom told me she visited a Gender Spectrum conference the year before. She learned all about trans children and care. She was ready to get me on puberty blockers or hormones. A few days after that discussion, I went to get clothes. My mom instinctively took me to the boy's section so I gave her a look and we both smiled. For the first time, I bought clothing from the girl's section. I didn't need to hide anymore: I could finally be myself.

The new school year went fast. I was noticeably happier and because of my now cheerful outlook, my community accepted me. They realized that letting me transition was the right thing to do and few questioned it. The harassment lessened because the community I lived in now knew why I acted the way I did. I experienced new forms of transphobic violence but now had the courage to fight back against it.

The next summer I attended my first trans conference. I met incredible teens and families who had gone through similar struggles that I had faced. I realized this was a community in which I belonged and I felt at home. After years of being alone, I could finally be myself around others like me. A few weeks later, right after my 15th birthday, I began hormones. I also intentionally kept my name: I didn't want to hide who I was. If someone asked, I would be proud to announce that I'm trans.

Over the next year, my confidence grew and I began to get more and more involved in the trans community. I began educating teachers about trans issues and took on more leadership roles. By that fall, in 11th grade, I started a transgender policy at my school that would have helped me while going through my town's education system. It didn't stop there. I then co-founded Trans Student Educational Resources with Chicago-based advocate Alex Sennello to engage with trans students, I became a GLSEN (Gay, Lesbian, and Straight Education Network) student media ambassador and National Advisory Council member, and I started presenting at queer conferences.

My parents went through changes of their own: my dad began speaking at trans conferences and my mom now helps run a local PFLAG chapter. I am incredibly privileged and grateful to have supportive parents and access to supportive medical care. We must recognize that many trans women of color often do not have these privileges, which is why their narratives must be centered in discussions of transness.

It is my hope is that we can create a world in which trans youth and their families have the strength to grow and change together.

Eli Erlick is an 18-year-old trans activist from California. She is the director of Trans Student Educational Resources, and a Gay, Lesbian, and Straight Education Network (GLSEN) National Advisory Council Member. You can follow Eli on Twitter at @eerlick

1. According to Eli Erlick, how did her gender identity affect her life?

2. Why was it hurtful for Eli's friends and family to initially deny her female self-identification?

EXCERPTS FROM "A SURVEY OF LGBT AMERICANS," FROM THE PEW RESEARCH CENTER, JUNE 13, 2013

ATTITUDES, EXPERIENCES, AND VALUES IN CHANGING TIMES

An overwhelming share of America's lesbian, gay, bisexual and transgender adults (92%) say society has become more accepting of them in the past decade and an equal number expect it to grow even more accepting in the decade ahead. They attribute the changes to a variety of factors, from people knowing and interacting with someone who is LGBT, to advocacy on their behalf by high-profile public figures, to LGBT adults raising families.

At the same time, however, a new nationally representative survey of 1,197 LGBT adults offers testimony to the many ways they feel they have been stigmatized by society. About four-in-ten (39%) say that at some point in their lives they were rejected by a family member or close friend because of their sexual orientation or gender identity; 30% say they have been physically attacked or threatened; 29% say they have been made to feel unwelcome in a place of worship; and 21% say they have been treated unfairly by an employer. About six-in-ten (58%) say they've been the target of slurs or jokes.

Also, just 56% say they have told their mother about their sexual orientation or gender identity, and 39% have told their father. Most who did tell a parent say that it was difficult, but relatively few say that it damaged their relationship.

The survey finds that 12 is the median age at which lesbian, gay and bisexual adults first felt they might be something other than heterosexual or straight. For those who say they now know for sure that they are lesbian, gay, bisexual or transgender, that realization came at a median age of 17.

Among those who have shared this information with a family member or close friend, 20 is the median age at which they first did so.

Gay men report having reached all of these coming out milestones somewhat earlier than do lesbians and bisexuals.

The survey was conducted April 11-29, 2013, and administered online, a survey mode that research indicates tends to produce more honest answers on a range of sensitive topics than do other less anonymous modes of survey-taking.

The survey finds that the LGBT population is distinctive in many ways beyond sexual orientation. Compared with the general public, Pew Research LGBT survey respondents are more liberal, more Democratic, less religious, less happy with their lives, and more satisfied with the general direction of the country. On average, they are younger than the general public. Their family incomes are lower, which may be related to their relative youth and the smaller size of their households. They are also more likely to perceive discrimination not just against themselves but also against other groups with a legacy of discrimination.

SOCIAL ACCEPTANCE AND THE PUBLIC'S PERSPECTIVE

Even though most LGBT adults say there has been significant progress toward social acceptance, relatively few (19%) say there is a lot of social acceptance for the LGBT population today. A majority (59%) says there is some, and 21% say there is little or no acceptance today.

Surveys of the general public show that societal acceptance is on the rise. More Americans now say they favor same-sex marriage and fewer say homosexuality should be discouraged, compared with a decade ago. These changing attitudes may be due in part to the fact that a growing share of all adults say they personally know someone who is gay or lesbian—87% today, up from 61% in 1993.

A new Pew Research Center analysis shows that among the general public, knowing someone who is gay or lesbian is linked with greater acceptance of homosexuality and support for same-sex marriage.

LGBT adults themselves recognize the value of these personal interactions; 70% say people knowing someone who is LGBT helps a lot in terms of making society more accepting of the LGBT population.

Still, a significant share of the public believes that homosexuality should be discouraged and that same-sex marriage should not be legal. Much of this resistance is rooted in deeply held religious attitudes, such as the belief that engaging in homosexual behavior is a sin.

And the public is conflicted about how the rising share of gays and lesbians raising children is affecting society. Only 21% of all adults say this trend is a good thing for society, 35%

say this is a bad thing for society, and 41% say it doesn't make much difference. The share saying this is a bad thing has fallen significantly in recent years (from 50% in 2007).

THE COMING OUT PROCESS

In the context of limited but growing acceptance of the LGBT population, many LGBT adults have struggled with how and when to tell others about their sexual orientation. About six-in-ten (59%) have told one or both of their parents, and a majority say most of the people who are important to them know about this aspect of their life.

Most of those who have told their parents say this process wasn't easy. Some 59% of those who have told their mother about their sexual orientation or gender identity and 65% who have told their father say it was difficult to share this information. However, of those who have told their mothers, the vast majority say it either made the relationship stronger (39%) or didn't change the relationship (46%). A similar-sized majority says telling their father about their sexual orientation or gender identity didn't hurt their relationship.

AGE, GENDER AND RACE

The survey finds that the attitudes and experiences of younger adults into the LGBT population differ in a variety of ways from those of older adults, perhaps a reflection of the more accepting social milieu in which younger adults have come of age.

For example, younger gay men and lesbians are more likely to have disclosed their sexual orientation somewhat earlier in life than have their older counterparts. Some of this difference may be attributable to changing social norms, but some is attributable to the fact that the experiences of young adults who have not yet identified as being gay or lesbian but will do so later in life cannot be captured in this survey.

As for gender patterns, the survey finds that lesbians are more likely than gay men to be in a committed relationship (66% versus 40%); likewise, bisexual women are much more likely than bisexual men to be in one of these relationships (68% versus 40%). In addition women, whether lesbian or bisexual, are significantly more likely than men to either already have children or to say they want to have children one day.

Among survey respondents, whites are more likely than non-whites to say society is a lot more accepting of LGBT adults now than it was a decade ago (58% vs. 42%) and, by a similar margin, are more optimistic about future levels of acceptance. Non-whites are more likely than whites to say being LGBT is extremely or very important to their overall identity (44% versus 34%) and more likely as well to say there is a conflict between their religion and their sexual orientation (37% versus 20%).

VIEWS OF ISSUES, LEADERS, INSTITUTIONS

On the eve of a ruling expected later this month by the U.S. Supreme Court on two same-sex marriage cases, 58% of LGBT adults say they have a favorable view of the court and 40% view it unfavorably; these assessments are similar to those held by the general public.

While the same-sex marriage issue has dominated news coverage of the LGBT population in recent years, it is only one of several top priority issues identified by survey respondents. Other top rank issues include employment rights, HIV and AIDS prevention and treatment, and adoption rights.

When asked in an open-ended question to name the national public figures most responsible for advancing LGBT rights, President Barack Obama, who announced last year that he had changed his mind and supports gay marriage, tops the list along with comedian and talk show host Ellen DeGeneres, who came out as a lesbian in 1997 and has been a leading advocate for the LGBT population ever since then. Some 23% of respondents named Obama and 18% named DeGeneres. No one else was named by more than 3% of survey respondents.

For the most part LGBT adults are in broad agreement on which institutions they consider friendly to people who are lesbian, gay, bisexual and transgender. Seven-in-ten describe the entertainment industry as friendly, 63% say the same about the Obama administration, and 57% view the Democratic Party as friendly. By contrast, just 4% say the same about the Republican Party (compared with 76% who say it is unfriendly); 8% about the military (47% unfriendly) and 4% about professional sports leagues (59% unfriendly). LGBT adults have mixed views about the news media, with 27% saying it is friendly, 56% neutral and 16% unfriendly.

LGBT survey respondents are far more Democratic than the general public—about eight-in-ten (79%) are Democrats or lean to the Democratic Party, compared with 49% of the general public. And they offer opinions on a range of public policy issues that are in sync with the Democratic and liberal tilt to their partisanship and ideology. For example, they are more likely than the general public to say they support a bigger government that provides more services (56% versus

40%); they are more supportive of gun control (64% versus 50%) and they are more likely to say immigrants strengthen the country (62% versus 49%).

SELF AND COUNTRY

LGBT adults and the general public are also notably different in the ways they evaluate their personal happiness and the overall direction of the country.

In the case of happiness, just 18% of LGBT adults describe themselves as "very happy," compared with 30% of adults in the general public who say the same. Gay men, lesbians and bisexuals are roughly equal in their expressed level of happiness.

When it comes to evaluations of the direction of the nation, the pattern reverses, with LBGT adults more inclined than the general public (55% versus 32%) to say the country is headed in the right direction. Opinions on this question are strongly associated with partisanship.

RELIGION

Religion is a difficult terrain for many LGBT adults. Lopsided majorities describe the Muslim religion (84%), the Mormon Church (83%), the Catholic Church (79%) and evangelical churches (73%) as unfriendly toward people who are LGBT. They have more mixed views of the Jewish religion and mainline Protestant churches, with fewer than half of LGBT adults describing those religions as unfriendly, one-in-ten describing each of them as friendly and the rest saying they are neutral.

The survey finds that LGBT adults are less religious than the general public. Roughly half (48%) say they have no religious affiliation, compared with 20% of the public at large. Of those LGBT adults who are religiously affiliated, one-third say there is a conflict between their religious beliefs and their sexual orientation or gender identity. And among all LGBT adults, about three-in-ten (29%) say they have been made to feel unwelcome in a place of worship. Pew Research surveys of the general public show that while societal views about homosexuality have shifted dramatically over the past decade, highly religious Americans remain more likely than others to believe that homosexuality should be discouraged rather than accepted by society. And among those who attend religious services weekly or more frequently, fully two-thirds say that homosexuality conflicts with their religious beliefs (with 50% saying there is a great deal of conflict). In addition, religious commitment is strongly correlated with opposition to same-sex marriage.

COMMUNITY IDENTITY AND ENGAGEMENT

As LGBT adults become more accepted by society, the survey finds different points of view about how fully they should seek to become integrated into the broader culture. About half of survey respondents (49%) say the best way to achieve equality is to become a part of mainstream culture and institutions such as marriage, but an equal share say LGBT adults should be able to achieve equality while still maintaining their own distinct culture and way of life.

Likewise, there are divisions between those who say it is important to maintain places like LGBT neighborhoods and bars (56%) and those who feel these venues will become less important over time (41%). Gay men are most likely of any of the LGBT subgroups to say that these distinctive venues should be maintained (68%).

When it comes to community engagement, gay men and lesbians are more involved than bisexuals in a variety of LGBT-specific activities, such as attending a gay pride event or being a member of an LGBT organization.

Overall, many LGBT adults say they have used their economic power in support or opposition to certain products or companies. About half (51%) say they have not bought a product or service because the company that provides it is not supportive of LGBT rights. A similar share (49%) says they have specifically bought a product or service because the company is supportive of LGBT rights.

Some 52% have attended an LGBT pride event, and 40% have attended a rally or march in support of LGBT rights. About four-in-ten (39%) say they belong to an LGBT organization and roughly three-in-ten (31%) have donated money to politicians who support their rights.

LGBT ADULTS ONLINE

LGBT adults are heavy users of social networking sites, with 80% of survey respondents saying they have used a site such as Facebook or Twitter. This compares with 58% of the general public (and 68% of all internet users), a gap largely attributable to the fact that as a group LGBT adults are younger than the general public, and young adults are much more likely than older adults to use social networking sites. When young LGBT adults are compared with all young adults, the share using these sites is almost identical (89% of LGBT adults ages 18 to 29 vs. 90% of all adults ages 18 to 29).

There are big differences across LGBT groups in how they use social networking sites. Among all LGBT adults, 55%

say they have met new LGBT friends online or through a social networking site. Gay men are the most likely to say they have done this (69%). By contrast, about half of lesbians (47%) and bisexuals (49%) say they have met a new LGBT friend online.

About four-in-ten LGBT adults (43%) have revealed their sexual orientation or gender identity on a social networking site. While roughly half of gay men and lesbians have come out on a social network, only about one-third (34%) of bisexuals say they have done this.

Just 16% say they regularly discuss LGBT issues online; 83% say they do not do this.

A NOTE ON TRANSGENDER RESPONDENTS

Transgender is an umbrella term that groups together a variety of people whose gender identity or gender expression differs from their birth sex. Some identify as female-to-male, others as male-to-female. Others may call themselves gender non-conforming, reflecting an identity that differs from social expectations about gender based on birth sex. Some may call themselves genderqueer, reflecting an identity that may be neither male nor female. And others may use the term transsexual to describe their identity. A transgender identity is not dependent upon medical procedures. While some transgender individuals may choose to alter their bodies through surgery or hormonal therapy, many transgender people choose not to do so.

People who are transgender may also describe themselves as heterosexual, gay, lesbian, or bisexual. In the Pew Research Center survey, respondents were asked whether they considered themselves to be transgender in a separate series of questions from the question about whether they considered themselves to be lesbian, gay, bisexual, or heterosexual.

The Pew Research survey finds that 5% of LGBT respondents identify primarily as transgender; this is roughly consistent with other estimates of the proportion of the LGBT population that is transgender. Although there is limited data on the size of the transgender population, it is estimated that 0.3% of all American adults are transgender (Gates 2011).

Because of the small number of transgender respondents in this survey (n=43), it is not possible to generate statistically significant findings about the views of this subgroup. However, their survey responses are represented in the findings about the full LGBT population throughout the survey.

The responses to both open- and closed-ended questions do allow for a few general findings. For example, among transgender respondents to this survey, most say they first felt their gender was different from their birth sex before puberty. For many, being transgender is a core part of their overall identity, even if they may not widely share this with many people in their lives.

And just as gay men, lesbians, and bisexuals perceive less commonality with transgender people than with each other, transgender adults may appear not to perceive a great deal of commonality with lesbians, gay men, and bisexuals. In particular, issues like same-sex marriage may be viewed as less important by this group, and transgender adults appear to be less involved in the LGBT community than are other sub-groups.

Here are some of the voices of transgender adults in the survey:

VOICES: TRANSGENDER SURVEY RESPONDENTS

ON GENDER IDENTITY

"It finally feels comfortable to be in my own body and head—I can be who I am, finally."
—Transgender adult, age 24

"I have suffered most of my life in the wrong gender. Now I feel more at home in the world, though I must admit, not completely. There is still plenty of phobic feeling."
—Transgender adult, age 77

"Though I have not transitioned fully, being born as male but viewing things from a female perspective gives me a perspective from both vantage points. I am very empathetic because of my circumstance."
—Transgender adult, age 56

"I wish I could have identified solely as male. Identifying as another gender is not easy."
—Transgender adult, age 49

ON TELLING PEOPLE

"Times were different for in-between kids born in the 30's. We mostly tried to conform and simply lived two lives at once. The stress caused a very high suicide rate and a higher rate of alcohol addiction (somehow I was spared both.)"
—Transgender adult, age 77

"It's been hard and very cleansing at the same time. The hardest part is telling old friends because they've known you for so long as your born gender. But most people are willing to change for you if they care enough."

—Transgender adult, age 27

"I have only told close members of my family and only a hand-ful of friends. I don't think that it is important to shout it out from the rooftops, especially in my profession."

—Transgender adult, age 38

"This process is difficult. Most people know me one way and to talk to them about a different side of me can be disconcerting. I have not told most people because of my standing in the com-munity and my job, which could be in jeopardy"

—Transgender adult, age 44

"Some of my family still refers to me as "she" but when we go out they catch themselves because of how I look, they sound foolish to strangers :). When it's a bunch of family or old friends, they usually don't assign me a gender they say my name. But I don't get too bothered by it, they are family and well, that's a huge thing to have to change in your mind. For the ones that do it out of disrespect, I just talk to them one on one and ask for them to do better."

—Transgender adult, age 29

1. According to the Pew Research Center, "transgender adults may appear not to perceive a great deal of commonality with lesbians, gay men, and bisexuals." Why?

"3 EXAMPLES OF EVERYDAY CISSEXISM," BY SIAN FERGUSON, FROM *EVERYDAY FEMINISM*, MARCH 21, 2014

Often, oppressive assumptions and myths are so embedded in our society that it is difficult to recognize how detrimental they are.

In order to effectively tackle inequality, **we must carefully examine the fundamental assumptions and attitudes that support oppression.**

Firstly, I want to point out that I'm cisgender.

I'm not a trans person, and as such, **I am definitely not the authority on what is cissexist and what is not.**

My aim here, however, is to educate others – *mainly other cisgender people* – and provoke discussion about cissexism within society.

I welcome any corrections, and am more than happy to listen to anyone who believes I did not check my cisgender privilege.

WHAT IS CISSEXISM?

We live in a society that assumes gender based on genitals. When we are born, we are categorized as a gender based on the appearance of our genitals.

"Transgender" is a word that generally refers to people who do not identify with the gender they were categorized as at birth.

A person with a penis would be classified as a boy, but will identify as a woman. Therefore, this person *is* a woman. Likewise, someone with a vagina might identify as a man.

Many people do not feel like solely a man or a woman. These people often refer to themselves as non-binary.

Trans* people can experience gender in a number of different ways.

As such, the existence of people who identify as transgender essentially challenges the idea that *gender = genitals.*

Unfortunately, the conflation of gender with genitals is deeply rooted in society.

It is seen as "normal" and "natural" to identify with the gender associated with one's genitals. As a result, **transgender people are often labelled unnatural or abnormal, and are oppressed, marginalized, and underrepresented by society.**

Cisgender people – *people who identify with the gender they were categorized as at birth* – enjoy a range of privileges over trans* folk.

We often use the word "transphobia" to refer to a range of negative attitudes towards trans* folk.

While the difference between cissexism and transphobia is not entirely clear, and many people use the terms interchangeably, **cissexism is often thought to be a more subtle form of transphobia.**

By "subtle," I mean that it is less visible to cisgender people. Despite this, **it is no less damaging.**

In fact, it could be argued that it is more damaging as fewer people notice it – while most decent people would be quick to condemn physical attacks on trans* folk, fewer people would notice how harmful it is to assume that only women have vaginas.

However, the very attitude that regards cisgender as the norm and others the trans* community leads to the denial of trans* people's rights.

Our society regularly makes cissexist assumptions.

It assumes that all people identify with the gender they were categorized as at birth, based on their genitals. Assuming all people are cisgender results in cisgender people being seen as "normal" and "natural," while transgender people are seen as the opposite – "abnormal" and "unnatural."

This attitude toward the trans* community is what leads to discrimination and transphobic attacks.

HOW SHOULD WE TACKLE CISSEXISM?

In order to eradicate transphobia, we need to tackle cissexism.

Questioning cissexism might seem like a difficult thing for cisgender people to do as it requires us to challenge our thinking at a very fundamental level. But it is still absolutely necessary.

Think about it: If challenging cissexism seems exhausting for us cisgender folk, how exhausting must it be to be a trans* person living in a cissexist society?

If we want to stand in solidarity with the trans* community – or be decent human beings – we *should* be prepared to do difficult work in order to challenge oppressive ideas.

That being said, **we're all socialized to be cissexist.**

So if you're working toward allyship and you *do* slip up once in a while, don't hate yourself for it. I used to wallow in my guilt every time I realized I had said something inadvertently racist, sexist, cissexist, ableist, or homophobic.

But guilt doesn't help anyone. Rather, it has a pacifying, negative effect on people.

Instead of overindulging in shame, I propose that we apologize, educate ourselves, and learn from the mistake so that we do not repeat it.

This allows us to continue to focus on the people we're trying to support, rather than our own feelings.

But beyond recognizing and owning up to our own mistakes, we can start tackling cissexism by taking a look at a few cissexist assumptions and dissecting them.

It is necessary for us to think about why they are harmful, how they contribute to cissexism, and how we can change it.

IDENTIFYING CISSEXISM

While the list of instances of cissexism is endless, I've decided to start by discussing three.

The assumptions in these situations are ones we've probably all made at some point in our lives (I know I still need to work on number three!). But it's important for us to work toward changing our attitudes, and those of people around us.

1) "IS IT A BOY OR A GIRL?"

This is one of the first questions that most people ask when they find out that someone is pregnant.

An idea that many people will find hard to wrap their heads around is that a sonogram will not be able to tell them what their child's gender is.

Since genitals do not determine gender, you actually won't know your child's gender identity until they're able to tell you.

To assume the child's gender based on their genitals is to assume that the child is cisgender.

This is a cissexist assumption – there is a chance that the child is trans*, and if this is the case, they should not feel othered.

I've found that plenty cisgender supporters of the trans* community assume their children to be cisgender, too.

This is an extremely difficult issue to navigate as raising a child without imposing a gender identity upon them is extremely tricky. Cissexism is so ingrained into our souls that we can hardly imagine freeing our children from it. It's a good idea to think about how we could make parenting less cissexist.

I don't know if I would ever have children, but if I did, I would raise them without choosing their gender identities for them. I don't think I would be able to reconcile my pro-trans* views with raising my child in a cissexist manner.

Also, ya know, I don't like the idea of defining my child by their genitals. Creepy!

2) SEXUAL EDUCATION

I'm a born-and-bred South African. While I can't speak for the rest of the world, I can safely say that the sexual education in South Africa is problematic. Heterosexism, impracticality, sexism, and slut-shaming aside, it is also extremely cissexist.

From a young age, we are taught that little girls have vaginas and little boys have penises. Later, we are taught about a "woman's reproductive system" and a "man's reproductive system."

In Life Orientation, we discuss women using oral contraception and men using condoms.

In all of these instances, gender is conflated with genitals.

Additionally, Life Sciences (biology) can espouse cissexism.

An over-simplified study of genetics tells us that women have XX chromosomes and that men have XY chromosomes. In reality, there are many instances in which people with XX chromosomes have penises and people with XY chromosomes have vaginas.

Even if the presence of XX chromosomes always resulted in the presence of a vagina, we know that not everyone with a vagina is a woman.

A simple addition to the curriculum could make a world of difference.

Schools are the perfect place to teach children and adolescents about transgender issues.

This being said, a change in curriculum seems a far-off dream for most of us. Instead, we can aim to educate the young people in our lives about trans* and intersex issues as best as we can.

When explaining genitals to smaller kids, explain that many women are born with penises, and that many boys are born with vaginas, and that many people are not men or women, or are a bit of both. And all of that is perfectly alright.

What matters is how one feels and identifies – not one's private parts.

Some people might want to change their bodies to reflect their gender identity, but some might not – and either way, it's perfectly okay.

When it comes to sexual education at a school level, we can talk about bodies typically associated with being male and those associated with being female.

We should explain that many people are born with ambiguous genitalia, which is usually referred to as intersex. This is perfectly okay, and this is natural.

Emphasize that genitals do not determine gender.

Many parents, teachers, and care-givers might be tempted to oversimplify and generalize when approaching sex ed.

They might simply tell their children/charges that boys have penises and girls have vaginas.

Even those who stand in solidarity with the trans* community might think that it would be better to simplify the message and allow the child to learn about transgender and intersex people later on in life.

Against this, M.A. Melby argues:

"What tying 'penis' to boys and 'vagina' to girls does is make genitalia part of what defines a 'boy' and a 'girl' for the child. Children are in the cognitive stage where they trust authority to define what things are, what is right and wrong, and what the fundamental models of the universe are."

She goes on to say that **teaching generalizations as the truth can be harmful.**

Most men have penises. Few women are presidents.

If we can justify teaching our children that *all* men have penises, we could use the same logic to justify teaching our daughters that *no* women ever become presidents.

If we wouldn't teach our children sexism, why would we teach them cissexism?

Teaching cissexism at an early stage will make it harder for children to change their thinking when they're older. This requires a lot of unlearning and relearning.

It would be a lot easier to simply nip cissexism in the bud by teaching your children the truth.

3) FEMINIST ACTIVISM

Lauren Kacere recently wrote about trans* exclusion in the feminist movement as well as how and why we should work toward making the movement trans-inclusive. Transphobia in feminism is a huge issue, but even seemingly trans-inclusive feminism **can be cissexist.**

Reproductive rights advocacy is an area where cissexist assumptions are often made.

Rights pertaining to abortion and contraception are often referred to as "women's reproductive rights." This is harmful as it assumes that the only people who need abortions are women.

By extension, it assumes that the only people who possess uteruses are women – another example of the conflation of genitals with gender.

This problem was identified by #ProTransProChoice campaign, which sought to encourage organisations such as Planned Parenthood and NARAL to use more trans-inclusive language.

As the campaign organizers point out in their change. org petition:

"The rhetoric of the pro-choice movement is typically based around the assumption that only folks who identify as women are hurt by restrictions on reproductive health care – such as abortion and contraception. #StandWithTexasWomen took the stage in 2013; 'Trust Women' has been the mantra of this movement for decades."

Often, pro-choice citizens complain about men dominating discussions about abortion, particularly in politics and law-making bodies. Many people argue that men should not have so much say over "women's" reproductive rights.

Let's remember that many men can fall pregnant, and they might need abortions.

Instead of simply saying that men should not dominate discussions about abortion, we should say that *cis* men should not dominate discussions about abortion.

Am I saying that pro-choice campaigns and organizations are transphobic? No – indeed, most reproductive rights advocacy appears to be very inclusive of the trans* community.

But the language they use, and the language the media and the public uses, needs to change to demonstrate that.

1. What do you think about the author's take on cissexism?

2. Do you think that people discriminate against transgender individuals without even realizing it?

CONCLUSION

After being considered a taboo subject by the public at large for a long time, the question of gender identity has gained a lot of attention recently due to transgender characters in popular TV shows and celebrities coming out as transgender. At the same time, efforts have been made by governments around the world to fight against discrimination, and numerous court cases show progress in this regard. Nonetheless, it seems that the so-called "tipping point" that some believe has been reached is still a bit off. Despite the increased visibility of transgender people in the media and recent political changes, prejudices are still common, and transgender people frequently face discrimination and even violence.

It would not be right to discount recent progress made in the arena of transgender rights. While there are still issues to be tackled, the acceptance of transgender people has increased and is likely to increase further thanks to the work of advocacy organizations and ordinary people who are taking a stand for equality and human rights. Perhaps recent scientific research pointing to brain structure as the potential cause of some transgender experience will help more people accept transgender individuals as who they are.

As other social movements have shown in the past, change can be a slow and painful process—often far slower than those hoping for change would like. The tipping point for the transgender movement may not yet be reached but the ongoing dialogue—as evidenced in this book—proves that society is on its way.

BIBLIOGRAPHY

American Psychological Association. "Answers to Your Questions About Transgender People, Gender Identity, and Gender Expression." 2011. Retrieved November 30, 2015 (www.apa.org/topics/lgbt/transgender.pdf).

Anderson, Dianna E. "Why Conservative Christians Fear the Affirmation of Transgender Identity." *RH Reality Check*, September 9, 2014. Retrieved November 30, 2015 (rhrealitycheck.org/article/2014/09/09/conservative-christians-fear-transgender-identity/).

Bindel, Julie. "The Operation That Can Ruin Your Life." *Standpoint Magazine*, November 2009. Retrieved November 30, 2015 (standpointmag.co.uk/node/2298/full).

Erlick, Eli. "I Knew I Was a Girl at 8: Transitioning and Teenage Activism." *Autostraddle,* September 30, 2013. Retrieved November 30, 2015 (http://www.autostraddle.com/i-knew-i-was-a-girl-at-8-transitioning-as-a-teenage-activist-197445/).

Ferguson, Sian. "3 Examples of Everyday Cissexism." *Everyday Feminism*, March 21, 2014. Retrieved November 30, 2015 (everydayfeminism.com/2014/03/everyday-cissexism/).

Friedman, Richard A. "How Changeable Is Gender?" *The New York Times*, August 22, 2015. Retrieved November 30, 2015 (nytimes.com/2015/08/23/opinion/sunday/richard-a-friedman-how-changeable-is-gender.html?_r=0).

Gender Spectrum. "Understanding Gender." Retrieved November 30, 2015 (www.genderspectrum.org/quick-links/understanding-gender/).

Germanos, Andrew. "US Hits Disturbing Milestone With Record High Number of Trasngender Murders." *Common Dreams,* November 13, 2013. Retrieved April 19, 2016 (http://www.commondreams.org/news/2015/11/13/us-hits-disturbing-milestone-record-high-number-transgender-murders).

Hammarberg, Thomas. "Human Rights and Gender Identity." July 29, 2009. Retrieved November 30, 2015 (wcd.coe.int/ViewDoc.jsp?id=1476365).

International Commission of Jurists. *Sexual Orientation, Gender Identity and Justice: A Comparative Law Casebook*. 2011. Retrieved November 30, 2015 (www.refworld.org/docid/4f9eae7c2.html).

Mottet, Lisa, and Justin Tanis. *Opening the Door to the Inclusion of Transgender People: The Nine Keys to Making Lesbian, Gay, Bisexual and Transgender Organizations Fully Transgender-Inclusive.* (New York: National Gay and Lesbian Task Force Policy Institute and the National Center for Transgender Equality, 2008).

Office of Personnel Management, the Equal Employment Opportunity Commission, the Office of Special Counsel, and the Merit Systems Protection Board. "Addressing Sexual Orientation and Gender Identity Discrimination in Federal Civilian Employment: A Guide to Employment Rights, Protections, and Responsibilities." Rev. June 2015. Retrieved November 30, 2015 (opm.gov/policy-data-oversight/diversity-and-inclusion/reference-materials/addressing-sexual-orientation-and-gender-identity-discrimination-in-federal-civilian-employment.pdf).

Pew Research Center. "A Survey of LGBT Americans." June 13, 2013. Retrieved April 19, 2016 (http://www.pewsocialtrends.org/2013/06/13/a-survey-of-lgbt-americans/).

"The Pope's Take on Transgender Issues? Accept the Body God Gave You." *Catholic News Agency,* June 18, 2015. Retrieved April 19, 2016 (http://www.catholicnewsagency.com/news/the-popes-take-on-transgender-issues-accept-the-body-god-gave-you-56797/).

Sasson, Eric. "America Has Not Reached a Transgender Tipping Point." *New Republic,* April 27, 2015. Retrieved November 30, 2015 (newrepublic.com/article/121653/bruce-jenner-interview-cox-photos-not-transgender-tipping-point).

St. James, James. "7 Trans Media Tropes That Need to Stop." *Everyday Feminism*, February 18, 2015. Retrieved November 30, 2015 (everydayfeminism.com/2015/02/trans-media-tropes/).

St. John, Paige. "In a first, California agrees to pay for transgender inmate's sex reassignment." *Los Angeles Times*, August 10, 2015. Retrieved November 30, 2015 (www.latimes.com/local/california/la-me-inmate-transgender-20150810-story.html).

Substance Abuse and Mental Health Services Administration. *A Practitioner's Resource Guide: Helping Families to Support Their LGBT Children*. HHS Publication No. PEP14-LGBTKIDS. Rockville, MD: Substance Abuse and Mental Health Services Administration, 2014.

US Equal Employment Opportunity Commission. "Fact Sheet: Recent EEOC Litigation Regarding Title VII & LGBT-Related Discrimination." Last Updated August 27, 2015. Retrieved November 30, 2015 (www.eeoc.gov/eeoc/litigation/selected/lgbt_facts.cfm).

US Office of Personnel Management. "Guidance Regarding the Employment of Transgender Individuals in the Federal Workplace." Retrieved November 30, 2015 (www.opm.gov/policy-data-oversight/diversity-and-inclusion/reference-materials/gender-identity-guidance/).

CHAPTER NOTES

CHAPTER 2: WHAT THE GOVERNMENT AND CHURCH LEADERS SAY

EXCERPT FROM "HUMAN RIGHTS AND GENDER IDENTITY," BY THOMAS HAMMARBERG

1. Definition as used in the Yogyakarta Principles on the Application of International Human Rights Law in relation to Sexual Orientation and Gender Identity, available at www.yogyakartaprinciples.org.
2. Ibid.
3. See also the Commissioner's Viewpoint "Discrimination against transgender persons must no longer be tolerated" published on 5 January 2009.
4. UN Committee on Economic, Social and Cultural Rights, General Comment No 20 on Non-Discrimination.
5. ECtHR, *van Kück v. Germany*, judgment of 12 June 2003.
6. ECtHR, *B. v. France*, judgment of 25 March 1992 and *Christine Goodwin v. U.K.*, judgment of 11 July 2002.
7. Sex discrimination has for long been included in relevant European Community legislation. Since 1957, the EEC Treaty has contained a provision prohibiting unequal pay for men and women, which has been revised in the Treaty of Amsterdam. From 1975, the EU has issued several directives on sex discrimination.
8. ECJ, Case C-13/94, *P. v. S. and Cornwall City Council,* judgment of 30 April 1996, ECR [1996] I-2143, ECJ, Case C-117/01, *K.B. v. National Health Service Pensions Agency, Secretary of State for Health,* judgment of 7 January 2004, ECJ, Case C-423/04, *Sarah Margaret Richards v Secretary of State for Work and Pensions,* judgment of 27.4.2006. See for an explanation of the progressive nature of the Judgements, European Union Agency for Fundamental Rights, Homophobia and Discrimination on the grounds of sexual orientation in the EU Member States, Part I Legal Analysis, p.124.
9. ECtHR, *B. v. France* judgment of 25 March 1992 (Series A no. 232-C) (distinguishing the Rees and Cossey judgments); *Sheffield and Horsham v. the United Kingdom* judgment of 30 July 1998; *Christine Goodwin v. the United Kingdom*, Appl. no.

28957/95, judgment of 11 July 2002; *Grant v. the United Kingdom*, Appl. no. 32570/03, judgment of 23 May 2006.

10. It is assessed that only 10% of all transgender persons actually choose, have access to or to are able to undergo gender reassignment surgery.

11. European Union Agency for Fundamental Rights, Homophobia and Discrimination on the grounds of sexual orientation in the EU Member States, Part I Legal Analysis, p.126.

12. See Council Directive 2004/113/EC of 13 December 2004 implementing the principle of equal treatment between men and women in the access to and supply of goods and services, OJ L 373, 21.12.2004, p.37; and Directive 2006/54/EC of the European Parliament and of the Council of 5 July 2006 on the implementation of the principle of equal opportunities and equal treatment of men and women in matters of employment and occupation (recast), OJ L 204 of 26.7.2006, p. 23 (Recast Gender Directive).

13. Statement of the Office of the UN High Commissioner for Human Rights to the International Conference on LGBT human rights, Montreal 26 July 2006, available at www.unhchr.ch/huricane/huricane.nsf/0/B91AE52651D33F0DC12571BE-002F172C?opendocument.

14. UN High Commissioner for Refugees, UNHCR Guidance Note on Refugee Claims Relating to Sexual Orientation and Gender Identity, 21 November 2008, available at: http://www.unhcr.org/refworld/docid/48abd5660.html.

15. Recommendation 1117 (1989) on the condition of transsexuals available at http://assembly.coe.int/main.asp?Link=/documents/adoptedtext/ta89/erec1117.htm.

16. Resolution on discrimination against transsexuals, Official Journal of the European Communities, C 256 , 09/10/1989, p 0033.

17. European Parliament resolution on homophobia in Europe (2006), available at www.europarl.europa.eu/sides/getDoc.do?type=TA&language=EN&reference=P6-TA-2006-0018; European Parliament resolution on homophobia in Europe (2007) available at www.europarl.europa.eu/sides/getDoc.do?pubRef=-//EP//TEXT+TA+P6-TA-2007-0167+0+DOC+XML+V0//EN.

18. Yogyakarta Principles on the Application of International Human Rights Law in relation to Sexual Orientation and Gender Identity, p. 11-12.

19. This is an initiative in which NGOs, job agencies and the city council work together.
20. Whittle, S; Turner, L (2007) Leading Trans Equality: A Toolkit for Colleges, Lancaster: The Centre for Excellence in Leadership, available at http://services.pfc.org.uk/files/CEL_toolkit.pdf.
21. To be who I am. Report of the Inquiry into Discrimination faced by transgender people, available at www.hrc.co.nz/hrc_new/hrc/cms/files/documents/21-Jan-2008_19-03-12_Transgender_Final_2.pdf.
22. Equality and Human Rights Commission (2008) Overview of the gender equality duty, Guidance for public bodies working in England, Wales and Scotland, available at www.equalityhumanrights.com.

CHAPTER 3: WHAT THE COURTS SAY

EXCERPT FROM "SEXUAL ORIENTATION, GENDER IDENTITY AND JUSTICE: A COMPARATIVE LAW CASEBOOK," FROM THE INTERNATIONAL COMMISSION OF JURISTS, 2011

1. For a critique of the heteronormativity of transgender legal arguments and jurisprudence, see David B. Cruz, "Getting Sex 'Right': The Heteronormativity and Biologism in Trans and Intersex Marriage Litigation and Scholarship," 18 Duke Journal Gender Law and Policy 203 (Fall 2010).
2. *Corbett v. Corbett* [1970], 2 All ER 33.
3. For a discussion of the influence of *Corbett*, see Andrew N. Sharpe, "From Functionality to Aesthetics: the Architecture of Transgender Jurisprudence," 8 Murdoch University Electronic Journal of Law (March 2011).
4. Sharpe, "From Functionality to Aesthetics: the Architecture of Transgender Jurisprudence," 8 Murdoch University Electronic Journal of Law (March 2001).
5. *Littleton v. Prange*, 9 S.W.3d 223 (Tex. App. 1999); *In re Estate of Gardiner*, 42 P.3d 120 (Kan. 2002); *In re Marriage License for Nash*, 2003, WL 23097095 (Ohio Ct. App. 2003); *Kantaras v.*

CRITICAL PERSPECTIVES ON GENDER IDENTITY

Kantaras; 884 So.2d 155 (Fla. Dist. Ct. App. 2004) (reversing opinion of trial court that had recognized validity of marriage); *In re Marriage of Simmons*, 825 N.E. 2d 303 (Ill. App. Ct. 2005).

6. *In re Marriage of Simmons*, 825 N.E.2d 303, 310 (holding that "the mere issuance of a new birth certificate cannot, legally speaking, make petitioner a male").

7. *M v. M*, [1991] NZFLR 337, Family Court Otahuhu (30 May 1991).

8. *M v. M*, [1991] NZFLR 337, Family Court Otahuhu (30 May 1991) at p. 35.

9. European Court of Human Rights, Judgment of 11 July 2002, *Goodwin v. United Kingdom*, Application No. 28957/95, at para. 77. See also European Court of Human Rights, Judgment of 11 July 2002, *I v. United Kingdom*, Application No. 256080/94, (finding violations of Articles 8 and 12 for refusal to grant legal recognition to individual following gender reassignment surgery).

10. Ibid., at *Goodwin v. United Kingdom*, para. 98.

11. Ibid., at para. 101.

12. Ibid., at para. 56.

GLOSSARY

cisgender—Opposite of transgender, a person whose gender identity conforms with the gender they were assigned at birth.

gender—Social construct of behaviors and traits typically associated with masculinity and femininity.

gender binary—The prevalent notion that there are only two genders, male and female, and that every person has to belong to one of these two categories.

gender dysphoria—A diagnosis described in the *Diagnostic and Statistical Manual of Mental Disorders* that can be applied to transgender people who experience their gender as distressing.

gender expression—A person's way of showing their gender identity through behavior, body characteristics, and outward appearance.

gender identity—A person's own concept of being male, female, or something other.

gender nonconforming—A person whose behavior and characteristics are perceived to be different from what society in general considers typical for a given gender.

genderqueer—A term for people who identify as being on the gender spectrum rather than one of the poles of the gender binary.

gender spectrum—A concept that views gender identity in a more complex and nuanced way than the gender binary.

intersex—A person with reproductive anatomy that is in-between male and female.

sex—The physical characteristics used to classify a person as male or female.

sexual orientation—A person's sexual attraction to other people based on the sex of the other person, which is not determined by their own gender identity.

CRITICAL PERSPECTIVES ON GENDER IDENTITY

trans*—The asterisk denotes the wide range of gender diversity in transgender individuals. Some trans activists use "trans*" instead of "transgender."

transgender—Adjective describing people whose gender identity differs from the sex they were assigned at birth.

transition—The social and medical process of changing one's gender so that it corresponds with one's gender identity.

transphobia—Fear of transgender people that often leads to discrimination and even violence.

transsexual—A person whose gender identity is the opposite of the gender they were assigned at birth.

FOR MORE INFORMATION

BOOKS

Andrews, Arin. *Some Assembly Required: The Not-So-Secret Life of a Transgender Teen*. New York, NY: Simon & Schuster BFYR, 2014.

Giordano, Simiona. *Children with Gender Identity Disorder: A Clinical, Ehtical, and Legal Analysis*. New York, NY: Routledge, 2013.

Kuklin, Susan. *Beyond Magenta: Transgender Teens Speak Out*. Somerville, MA: Candlewick Press, 2014.

Meyer, Elizabeth J., and Dennis Carlson (eds.). *Gender and Sexualities in Education*. New York, NY: Peter Lang, 2014.

Meyer, Elizabeth J., and Pullen Sansfaçon. *Supporting Transgender & Gender Creative Youth: Schools, Families, and Communities in Action*. New York, NY: Peter Lang, 2014.

Miller, Beverly L. (ed.). *Gender Identity: Disorders, Developmental Perspectives and Social Implications*. Hauppauge, NY: Nova Science Publishers, 2014.

Rupp, Leila J., and Susan K. Freeman. *Understanding and Teaching U.S. Lesbian, Gay, Bisexual, and Transgender History*. Madison, WI: The University of Wisconsin Press, 2014.

Scherpe, Jens M. *The Legal Status of Transsexual and Transgender Persons*. Cambridge, UK: Intersentia, 2014.

Testa, Rylan Jay, Deborah Coolhart, and Jayme Peta. *The Gender Quest Workbook: A Guide for Teens and Young Adults Exploring Gender Identity*. Oakland, CA: New Harbinger Publications, 2015.

Yarhouse, Mark A. *Understanding Gender Dysphoria: Navigating Transgender Issues in a Changing Culture*. Downers Grove, IL: IVP Academic, 2015.

WEBSITES

Gender Spectrum

www.genderspectrum.org

Gender Spectrum aims to help people understand the concept of gender identity and offers consultation, training, and events to that end.

The Human Rights Campaign

www.hrc.org

The Human Rights Campaign is the biggest civil rights organization working toward equality for lesbian, gay, bisexual, and transgender Americans, and its website offers news and original reports on related topics.

The National Center for Transgender Equality

www.transequality.org

The National Center for Transgender Equality covers a lot of issues from antiviolence to voting rights for transgender people.

INDEX

A

"Addressing Sexual Orientation and Gender Identity Discrimination in Federal Civilian Employment: A Guide to Employment Rights, Protections, and Responsibilities," 54–69

advocacy groups, views on gender identity, 109–133

advocate, being a, 20

Alcorn, Leelah, 138

"America Has Not Reached a Transgender Tipping Point," 135–138

American Psychological Association, 9–20

Anderson, Dianna E., 72–78

"Answers to Your Questions About Transgender People, Gender Identity, and Gender Expression," 9–20

anti-discrimination laws, 18, 20, 45, 47, 128, 137

anxiety, 7, 17, 27, 104

Autostraddle, 160–166

B

Bindel, Julie, 139–146

body dysmorphic disorder, 145

C

Catholic News Agency, 69–72

celebrities, transgender, 7, 73, 134, 135–136

Christians, conservative, 72–78

Christine Goodwin v. United Kingdom, 88–90

church leaders, views on gender identity, 40, 69–78

cisgender people, 6, 74, 114, 117, 150–151, 153, 154, 155, 156, 157, 159–160, 180, 181–182, 184, 188

cissexism, 180–188

coming out, 29–30, 31–32, 33, 168, 170–171

Common Dreams, 147–149

Corbett v. Corbett, 81, 82, 83, 86, 87, 88, 89

Council of Europe Commissioner for Human Rights, the Council of Europe, 39, 40–53

counseling, 17, 131

courts, decisions on gender identity, 79–108

Cox, Laverne, 73, 135–136, 138

cross-dressing, 12, 41, 45, 129

D

DeGeneres, Ellen, 136, 172

depression, 7, 8, 17, 25, 27, 35, 104

Dhejne, Cecilia, 24

Diagnostic and Statistical Manual of Mental Disorders (DSM-5), 17

discrimination of transgender people, 7, 9, 17, 18–19, 25, 39, 41, 43, 44–46, 49, 50, 54–62, 73–75, 79, 92–102, 121, 137, 181, 182, 189

drag kings and queens, 12

E

education issues, 18, 131–132, 161–162, 163–164, 165

employment, 7, 48–49
discrimination in, 18, 54–62, 74, 79, 92–102, 121, 137
guidance for employers regarding, 62–69

Equal Employment Opportunity Commission, U.S., 39, 54–69, 91–102
Erlick, Eli, 160–166
European Commissioner for Human Rights, 39
European Court for Human Rights, 44, 45, 89–90
Everyday Feminism, 149–158, 180–188
experts, views on gender identity, 8–38

F
"Fact Sheet: Recent EEOC Litigation Regarding Title VII & LGBT-related Discrimination," 91–102
Ferguson, Sian, 180–188
Francis, Pope, 69–72
Friedman, Richard A., 8, 21–29

G
Gay Straight Alliance, 37
gender
    difference between gender and sex, 10, 41, 110
    privilege and, 114–115, 180
    spectrum of, 111, 164
    terminology, 115–117
    understanding, 110–117
gender affirmation, 11, 15, 20
gender dysphoria, 103, 104, 140, 141, 145, 146
    in children, 26–27, 160–161
    diagnosis and treatment of, 8, 17, 21
gender expansiveness, 112–113
gender expression, 9, 12, 18, 42, 112, 114, 115–116, 117, 122, 128, 131, 137, 161, 176
gender fluidity, 117

gender identity, 13, 18, 41–42, 56, 63, 114, 115, 116, 122, 128, 131, 137, 176, 184
    age it's often expressed, 32, 115, 143
    recent visibility of issue, 7, 73, 134, 135–136, 142–143, 149, 189
    relationship between gender identity and sexual orientation, 13–14
gender identity disorder, 18
genderqueer people, 12, 129, 176
gender reassignment, 11, 24, 25, 27, 44–45, 49, 52, 63, 81, 83, 84, 86, 88, 103–108, 140–142
gender roles, 15, 21, 23, 32, 67, 110, 112, 116, 139–140
Gender Spectrum, 110–117
Germanos, Andrew, 147–149
government, views on gender identity, 39–69
Grace, Laura Jane, 73
Green, Richard, 26

H
Hammarberg, Thomas, 40–53
hate crimes, 19, 52
health care, 18, 128, 130–131, 147
homelessness, 34, 137
homophobia, 43, 120–121, 123, 136
hormone therapy, 16, 17, 20, 21, 22, 25, 27, 41, 48, 52, 63, 81, 84, 85, 88, 104, 106, 107, 115, 130, 141, 143, 146, 164, 176
housing, discrimination in, 18
"How Changeable Is Gender?," 21–29
"Human Rights and Gender Identity," 40–53

I

"I Knew I Was a Girl at 8: Transitioning and Teenage Activism," 160–166

"In a First, California Agrees to Pay for Transgender Inmate's Sex Reassignment," 103–108

"Injustice at Every Turn," 18

inmates, prison, 103–108, 144

In re Kevin, 85–86, 87, 90

In re Love-Lara, 83

In re Simmons, 83

insurance, 7, 52, 68, 128, 130–131, 137, 153

International Classification of Diseases (ICD), 17–18

International Commission of Jurists, 80–90

intersex conditions, 10, 40, 44, 186

J

Jenner, Caitlyn (Bruce), 21, 135, 136

K

Kosilek, Michelle, 107

Kranz, Georg S., 21–22

L

legal systems, discrimination in, 18

LGBT

acceptance and inclusion of transgender people, 118–133

coming out and self-awareness, 29–30, 31–32, 33, 168, 170–171

community identity and engagement, 174–175

family not accepting of, 32–35, 36–37

greater awareness and visibility of, 29, 32

online activity, 175–176

religion and, 173–174

social acceptance of, 167–170, 172, 174

support for, 30–31, 33, 34, 35–37

survey of, 167–179

Los Angeles Times, 103–108

M

marriage, issues of, 48, 52, 68, 75, 77, 79, 80–90, 124, 136, 169, 171, 172, 174

Masbruch, Sherri, 106

media, views on gender identity, 134–158

mental health professionals, 16, 20, 25, 52, 130

Merit Systems Protection Board, 39, 54–69

military and transgender people, 21, 172

Mottet, Lisa, 118–133

MT v. JT, 81–82, 83, 84, 87

murders of transgender people, 147–149

M v. M, 83–84

N

name, changing, 49–50, 52, 65–66, 67, 68, 106, 130

National Center for Transgender Equality, 18, 118–133

National Gay and Lesbian Task Force, 18, 136

Policy Institute, 118–133

New Republic, 135–138

New York Times, 21–29

O

Obama, Barack, 74, 107, 138, 172

Office of Personnel Management, 39, 54–69

Office of Special Counsel, 39, 54–69

"Opening the Door to the Inclusion of Transgender People: The Nine Keys to Making Lesbian, Gay, Bisexual and Transgender Organizations Fully Transgender Inclusive," 118–133

"Operation That Can Ruin Your Life, The," 139–146

P

parents/families of transgender children, 15, 18, 161–162, 163–166

Pejic, Andreja, 135, 136

Pew Research Center, 167–179

"Pope's Take on Transgender Issues? Accept the Body God Gave You, The," 69–72

"Practioner's Resource Guide: Helping Families to Support Their LGBT Children, A," 29–38

pronouns and names, using appropriate, 19, 23, 65–66, 99, 130, 135

puberty suppression, 27, 143, 164

Q

Quine, Shiloh, 103–107

R

race issues, transgender people and, 19, 101, 147, 148, 152–153, 171

religious communities
  affiliation of LGBT people, 173–174
  views on gender identity, 40, 69–78
  views on homosexuality, 169, 173–174

reparative therapy, 23, 28, 161

restrooms, 7, 66–67, 92, 109, 114, 130, 137

RH Reality Check, 72–78

S

Sasson, Eric, 135–138

"7 Trans Media Tropes That Need to Stop," 149–158

sex and gender, difference between, 10, 41, 110

sexual orientation, 12, 13, 20, 23, 56, 98, 116, 128
  discrimination in employment, 54–62, 100–101
  human rights and, 42–47
  relationship between sexual orientation and gender identity. 13–14, 116
  reparative therapy and, 23, 28

"Sexual Orientation, Gender Identity and Justice: A Comparative Law Casebook," 80–90

shame, feelings of, 14, 164

society, views on gender identity, 135–136, 180–188

Southern Baptist Convention, 72–74

Standards of Care for Gender Identity Disorders, The, 17

Standpoint Magazine, 139–146

St. James, James, 149–158

St. John, Paige, 103–108

stress, 8, 18

substance abuse, 35

Substance Abuse and Mental Health Services Administration, 29–38

suicide, 25, 34, 35, 37, 104, 105, 107, 137, 178

support groups, 16, 20, 37, 49

surgery, 21, 25, 41, 44, 48, 49, 52, 63, 81, 83, 84, 85, 86, 88, 103–108, 115, 135, 139–146, 153, 176

"Survey of LGBT Americans," 167–179

T

Tanis, Justin, 118–133

"3 Examples of Everyday Cissexim," 180–188

Title VII, 91–102

transgender community, 16, 26, 165

transgender people

acceptance of, 7, 21, 23, 33, 35, 118–113, 149, 164–166, 167, 189

categories of, 11–13, 41

defined, 6–7, 9–10, 40, 63, 116, 142, 176, 180–181

discrimination/ostracizing of, 7, 9, 17, 18–19, 25, 39, 41, 43, 44–46, 49, 50, 54–62, 73–75, 79, 92–102, 121, 137, 181, 182, 189

family not accepting of, 32–35, 36–37, 161–162, 164

feelings of not "fitting in," 14–15, 114–115

history of, 11–13

how people know they are transgender, 14–15

how they transition, 16–17

human rights and, 40–53

is it a mental disorder?, 17–18, 42

prevalence of, 13, 24, 177

recent visibility, 7, 73, 134, 135–136, 142–143, 149, 189

statistics on, 24, 25, 137

support for, 9, 15, 17, 19–20, 23, 35–37, 49, 109–110, 124–133

survey of, 177–179

views on gender identity, 159–166, 167–179

why some people are transgender, 13, 22–23

transitioning, 14, 16–17, 20, 63–68, 92, 93, 96, 137, 140, 152–153, 163, 165

transphobia, 9, 43, 73, 123, 125, 138, 144, 145, 148, 165, 181, 182, 187

transsexuals, 11, 15, 16, 22, 24–25, 40, 41, 44, 47, 51, 85, 86–87, 93, 99, 139, 140–141, 142, 143–146, 176

TV shows/movies, transgender people/characters in, 7, 134, 149–158, 189

U

"Understanding Gender," 110–117

"US Hits Disturbing Milestone with Record High Number of Transgender Murders," 147–149

V

violence against LGBT people, 7, 9, 17, 25, 41, 43, 45–46, 72–73, 105, 120, 121, 129–130, 132, 137, 147–149, 156, 165, 182, 189

W

Wachowski, Lana, 73

Wallein, Madeleine S. C., 26

"Why Conservative Christians Fear the Affirmation of Transgender Identity," 72–78

World Professional Association for Transgender Health (WPATH), 16–17

W v. Registrar of Marriages, 86–88

ABOUT THE EDITOR

Dr. Nicki Peter Petrikowski is a literary scholar as well as an editor, author and translator.